Strategic Planning for Sustainability

Strategic Planning for Sustainability

Alan S. Gutterman

BEP

BUSINESS EXPERT PRESS

Leader in applied, concise business books

Strategic Planning for Sustainability

Cover design by Charlene Kronstedt

Interior design by Exeter Premedia Services Private Ltd., Chennai, India

First published in 2021 by
Business Expert Press, LLC
222 East 46th Street, New York, NY 10017
www.businessexpertpress.com

ISBN-13: 978-1-95253-894-0 (paperback)
ISBN-13: 978-1-95253-895-7 (e-book)

Business Expert Press Environmental and Social Sustainability
for Business Advantage Collection

Collection ISSN: 2327-333X (print)
Collection ISSN: 2327-3348 (electronic)

First edition: 2021

10 9 8 7 6 5 4 3 2 1

Printed in the United States of America.

Description

Although corporate social responsibility (CSR) has been adopted by many companies, few of them are practicing it with any formal strategy, and the common situation seems to be a portfolio of disparate CSR programs and initiatives, some of which the support core strategy and others of which appear adjacent and discretionary. The diversity of potential CSR initiatives is one issue (e.g., companies may simultaneously disburse funding for community activities, provide grants for nonprofits or nongovernmental organizations (NGOs), launch environmental sustainability programs to reduce energy and resource use and engage in "cause" marketing and comprehensive system-level efforts to remake their entire value chain); however, developing a strategic orientation is complicated by the fact that each company has its own unique set of drivers and motivations for CSR and ideas and responsibilities for those initiatives come from all parts and levels of the organization. Moreover, while it makes sense to identify a specific business logic and rationale for each CSR initiative, the reality is that companies often take on causes and projects that have little or no connection to their core competencies or business strategy. A serious interest in CSR strategy has been driven by the emergence of two challenging environmental conditions that must now be addressed by all companies: the growing interest in sustainability and the need to engage with a broad range of stakeholders beyond the owners of the business. These conditions have not made strategic planning any easier, given that they expand the levels of unpredictability and risk in any company's environment, and the response has been the development of a new discipline: strategic planning for sustainability. Strategic planning for sustainability is far from easy or precise, if only because it requires that simultaneous consideration be given not only to economic performance and development but also to environmental protection and the social well-being of employees and other persons and groups outside of the organization. Companies and their managers are struggling to find and deploy the tools and practices that are necessary for balancing and reconciling the "triple bottom line" of profits, planet, and people. This book is intended as a comprehensive guide to the key steps required to strategically approach becoming a successful sustainable business including conducting a CSR assessment, developing a CSR strategy and the accompanying business case, developing and implementing CSR commitments, and measuring the performance and effectiveness of the planning initiative.

Keywords

strategy; strategic planning; sustainability; triple bottom line; CSR

Contents

Chapter 1   Introduction 1

Chapter 2   Environmental Forces and Strategic Planning.................25

Chapter 3   Conducting a CSR Assessment......................................49

Chapter 4   Developing a Corporate Social Responsibility
                   Strategy 67

Chapter 5   Developing CSR Commitments.....................................89

Chapter 6   Implementing CSR Commitments...............................111

Chapter 7   Measuring Planning Performance and Effectiveness......143

About the Author..163

Index 165

CHAPTER 1

Introduction

In order to understand how to formulate and execute a strategy for corporate social responsibility (CSR) and sustainability, it is necessary to have a foundation in the art and science of strategic planning generally. A substantial amount of literature exists on the importance of strategic planning and it generally is accepted that implementing and maintaining formal planning processes at the appropriate time during the development of the company is an essential element in creating and maintaining competitive advantage. It is not uncommon for larger companies to employ teams of experts in a dedicated strategic planning unit to work full-time on the planning process and to solicit input from hundreds or thousands of managers throughout the organization. For smaller companies, however, the process is necessarily more informal and compressed and may even be as simple as the founder or chief executive officer (CEO) sitting down with a handful of key employees to solicit their opinions on where the company should go over the planning period and what investments will need to be made in order to achieve the mutually recognized goals and objectives.

Regardless of the context, a variety of factors determine the planning practices that may be adopted by a particular company including environmental conditions, which include both the "specific environment" (i.e., the forces, such as stakeholders, that can be expected to have a direct impact on the ability of the specific company to obtain the scarce resources required for the company to create value for its owners and other stakeholders); and the "general environment" (i.e., the forces that typically will have an impact on the shape and design of all companies, including the company and other companies that are part of the stakeholder network of the company (e.g., economic, technological, political, demographic and socio-cultural forces)); organizational size, complexity and age; the nature of the business engaged in by the firm, top management values and styles; organizational culture; and the initial trigger for commencement of formal planning.[1]

Definitions and Objectives of Strategic Planning

Simply put, strategic planning can be thought of as a process of carefully and thoughtfully aligning the strengths of a company's business to the opportunities that are available to the company in its chosen business environment. While strategic planning is much debated and remains imprecise in many ways, it is generally believed that in order for this process to be successful the managers of the company must collect, screen, and analyze information about the company's business environment, identify and evaluate the strengths and weaknesses of the company, and develop a clear mission for the company and a set of achievable goals and objectives that then become the basis for tactical and operational plans. The strategic planning process allows managers to be proactive in identifying, and

---

[1] Brews, P., and M. Hunt. 1999. "Learning to Plan and Planning to Learn: Resolving the Planning School/Learning School Debate." *Strategic Management Journal* 20, no. 10, pp. 889–913; Miller, C., and L. Cardinal. 1994. "Strategic Planning and Firm Performance: A Synthesis of More Than Two Decades of Research." *Academy of Management Journal* 37, no. 6, pp. 1649–1665; Goll, I., and A. Rasheed. 1997. "Rational Decision-Making and Firm Performance: The Moderating Role of Environment." *Strategic Management Journal* 18, no. 7, pp. 583–591; Anchor, J., and J. Dehayyat. 2010. *Organisational Characteristics and Strategic Planning in an Emerging Economy: the Case of Jordan*. Huddersfield, UK: Unpublished Working Paper. Emerging Markets Research Group University of Huddersfield, http://eprints.hud.ac.uk/7504/ (citing, e.g., Greenley, G. 1986. "Does Strategic Planning Improve Company Performance?" *Long Range Planning* 19, no. 2, 101–108; Schwenk, C., and C. Schrader. 1993. "Effects of Formal Planning on Financial Performance in Small Firms: A Meta-Analysis." *Entrepreneurship Theory and Practice* 17, no. 3, pp. 56–63; Powell, T. 1994. "Untangle the Relationship between Strategic Planning and Performance: The Role of Contingency Factors." *Canadian Journal of Administrative Science* 11, no. 2, pp. 124–144; Hopkins, W., and S. Hopkins. 1997. "Strategic Planning-Financial Performance Relationships in Banks: A Causal Examination." *Strategic Management Journal* 18, no. 8, pp. 635–652; and Rudd, J., G. Greenley, A. Beatson and I. Lings. 2008. "Strategic Planning and Performance: Extending the Debate." *Journal of Business Research* 61, pp. 99–108).

responding to, changes in the company's business environment. Companies can use strategic planning to prepare for future events and allocate their resources to take advantage of emerging opportunities and minimize the potential harm from environmental threats such as new competitors and technologies and changes in customer requirements or regulatory guidelines. Strategic planning is an important and essential process for every company regardless of the size of its business and the time and other resources the company has available to invest in the developing, documenting, implementing, and monitoring a strategic plan. The business environment and relevant technologies are constantly changing and new risks and uncertainties will surface on a regular basis.

Management Participation in the Planning Process

In order for strategic planning to be successful and meaningful, there must be active and enthusiastic participation from multiple levels of management within the firm in order to bring the most experience to the planning process and ensure that plans are made based on the full and current information about the operational activities of the firm and conditions in the marketplace. Managers at the highest level of the company—the CEO and the senior executives of all of the key functional groups and other business units—are charged with defining the strategic mission of the company and selecting and articulating the company's overriding goals and objectives. Other members of the management group are responsible for collecting the information that the executive group needs in order to engage in long range planning, which usually means reports that include necessary data about operations, finances, competitive conditions, technological trends, and other important characteristics of the external environment in which the firm is operating.

Active involvement of all managers throughout the company in the planning process is also required because a company's strategy is not only firmwide goals and objectives but also a comprehensive set of tactical and operational plans that impact the activities of everyone inside the company. While senior executives should expect to pore over and digest mountains of information about every aspect of the company's business their key role is to establish general, long-term goals, and objectives for the firm that will usually take more than just one annual planning period to achieve (e.g., long-term growth of revenues, market share or product lines; improved profitability; and/or building a "best of class" customer service function). It then falls on the managers of each business unit and department to identify and implement the specific ideas, or tactics, that are best suited to achieving the goals and objectives set at the top of the company. These tactical plans address important and practical questions for each unit or department: what needs to be done, how it will be done, what resources are needed to do it, how will those resources be acquired and managed, and how will progress be tracked and evaluated. Tactical plans typically cover one year or less and require the same type of information needed to set overall goals and objectives—financial information, operational performance data, and information on markets and the external environment in general. The supervisors below the business unit and departmental managers also play an important role in the strategic planning process by the way in which they develop and enforce the operational plans that serve as guides for the day-to-day activities of the specific employees that they oversee. The supervisors are responsible for the "nuts and bolts" of executing the tactical plans and do so through scheduling, budgeting, setting, and enforcing standards (i.e., policies, procedures, methods, and rules) and identifying and procuring necessary resources (e.g., personnel, information, capital, facilities, machinery, equipment, and materials).

The recognition that planning is a collaborative exercise may require some changes in the company's management style and company culture. In order to create and implement the most effective strategy, managers must be open to innovation, change, and new ways of doing business and communicating. Specifically, management must be willing to accept and embrace employee participation and set up a whole set of procedures and practices that support the planning process. For example, if the plan includes performance targets, appropriate changes in the incentive and reward systems in the firm may be required. If the traditional approach to decision making within the company has been "top-down" and managers and employees at lower levels of the organizational hierarchy have simply accepted directives from the senior management team without question or advance consultation, it can be expected that the transition to collaborative planning will be difficult. There may be deep reservoirs of distrust and fear that will depress the flow of new ideas and critical feedback that is so necessary to effective planning.

Fundamental Elements of the Planning Process

Strategic planning has become increasingly complicated with the introduction of new theories and supporting technologies that attempt to incorporate the seemingly unlimited number of variables that firms must consider when grappling with the challenge of anticipating future changes in their external environment. However, the fundamental elements of the planning process—the key initial steps and activities—have generally remained the same and thus provide a roadmap for the leaders of any company to launch and maintain their strategic planning activities:

- Define the mission of the firm, which is a statement of the purpose of the company typically described in a formal "mission statement." The mission statement should be clear and concise summary, generally no more than a single sentence, which summarizes what the firm does and provides direction for managers and employees as the types of decisions that should be made with respect to the operational activities of the company and the opportunities that should be pursued. A mission statement is not effective unless each employee is able to recite it from memory.
- Conduct a comprehensive SWOT (Strengths, Weaknesses, Opportunities, and Threats) analysis to develop the foundation for the strategic plan. This type of analysis forces the management team to make a thorough internal assessment of the company's distinctive competences and the areas in which the company lags behind competitors and/or is unprepared for identifiable changes in the business environment. An external assessment is also required to identify strengths and weaknesses of competitors, emerging technologies, and changes in customer habits and requirements.
- Define strategic goals and objectives, which are the performance milestones that must be attained in order for the company to

advance from its current position—identified in the SWOT analysis—to the position suggested by its mission statement. Goals and objectives are both quantitative—return on investment, earnings per share, gross revenues, profit margin, and market share—and qualitative—improve workforce skills and implement best practices for project management and operations, and must be defined in such a way that progress can be tracked and evaluated. Whenever possible, the key strategic goals and objectives should be succinctly summarized in a short strategy statement that becomes as familiar to all managers and employees as the mission statement.

- Develop tactical plans based on the selected goals and objectives of the company and operational plans that support execution of the elements of the tactical plans. Tactical and operational planning is necessary in order to ensure that managers and employees at every level in the company act in a manner that is consistent with pursuit of the company's strategic goals and objectives.
- Develop processes for continuously monitoring the effectiveness of the plan and identifying changes in the company's business environment. Monitoring is done to ensure that the plan is being executed correctly and to uncover methods for improving the planning process. In addition, monitoring is the best and only way to really identify when changes in the plan, as well as the company's overall strategic goals and objectives, are needed. Information collected from the monitoring processes should be used as valuable input for the next planning cycle.

Formal strategies should be created for the purpose of defining and pursuing ambitious long-term goals and objectives—targets that the firm wishes to achieve by certain dates that fall outside of the usual short-term planning period of 6 to 12 months. The time period to be covered by the strategic planning process should be dictated by the length of time that the company is willing and able to commit its current resources. Strategic plans typically extend no longer than five years and may go out only two or three years for many emerging companies given the dynamic rate of change in their business environments and the fact that their limited resources at the time of launch demand a focus on goals and objectives that can reasonably be achieved within a relatively short period of time in order to survive and attract additional resources. Strategic planning has usually been done on an annual basis with planning activities concentrated into several weeks or months immediately prior to the beginning on each annual planning period (e.g., for companies operating under calendar year plans and budgets the planning process would be scheduled for October and/or November prior the beginning of the year to be covered by the plan). However, many firms, particularly emerging companies operating in dynamic environments in which changes can and do occur quickly, have abandoned their annual plans in favor of continuous planning processes that make it easier for the company to readily identify new opportunities and make the necessary changes in course required to take advantage of them.

Strategic Planning for Sustainability

Corporate sustainability and social responsibility initiatives had been subject to criticism from both sides of the ideological spectrum.[2] On the left advocates from civil society have often questioned the fundamental motivations of corporations' actions under the umbrella of CSR, arguing that in most cases corporate support for environmental and social programs was nothing more than a public relations campaign designed primarily, if not solely, to boost brand reputations as another means for achieving the primary corporate objective of maximizing profits. At the other end of the spectrum, CSR has been denounced as inappropriate and unnecessary in a capitalist society where the responsibility of business is to create financial returns for its shareholders and the larger economy and environmental and social issues should be left to the government and civil society. Both sides have also complained about the lack of metrics to evaluate the efficacy of CSR programs, a situation that is all the more problematic given that businesses are generally driven and managed through precise

---

[2] Rangan, K., L. Chase, and S. Karim. 2012. "Why Every Company Needs a CSR Strategy and How to Build It." Cambridge MA: Harvard Business School Working Paper 12–088, April 5.

tools designed to track and analyze the performance of every investment decision.[3]

In spite of the criticisms, sustainability and CSR have become mainstays of business activities: the percentage of large global companies professing to practice some form of sustainability and CSR has been steadily increasing, sustainability reporting has become the norm and businesses of all sizes are subject to sustainability and CSR drivers including the philanthropic motivations of their employees and the expectations of other stakeholders such as customers and investors. As such, sustainability management now includes finding a way to forge a coherent strategy that can accommodate a broad range of sustainability and CSR activities including corporate funding of community activities, grants for nonprofits/nongovernment organizations (NGOs), environmental sustainability programs to reduce energy and resource use, "cause" marketing, and comprehensive system-level efforts to remake a business's entire value chain.[4]

Rangan et al. argued that while they believed that every company needed a sustainability and CSR strategy, few of the many companies that had already adopted sustainability were practicing it with a formal strategy. They found that the common situation was a portfolio of disparate sustainability and CSR programs and initiatives, some of which supported core strategy and others of which appeared adjacent and discretionary.[5] The diversity of sustainability and CSR activities cited earlier is one issue; however, developing a strategic orientation is complicated by the fact that each company has its own unique set of drivers and motivations for sustainability and CSR and ideas and responsibilities for those

---

[3] On the ideological debate over CSR, see Karnani, A. Winter 2011. "Doing Well by Doing Good: The Grand Illusion." *California Management Review*, 53; and Windsor, D. 2006. "Corporate Social Responsibility: Cases For and Against." In Epstein, M. and Hanson, K. (eds.), *The Accountable Corporation: Corporate Social Responsibility*, Vol 3, 41–43. Westport, CT: Praeger Publishers.

[4] Rangan, K., L. Chase, and S. Karim. April 5, 2012. "Why Every Company Needs a CSR Strategy and How to Build It." Cambridge MA: Harvard Business School Working Paper 12–088

[5] See also Googins, B., and S. Rochlin. 2006. "Corporate Citizenship Top to Bottom: Vision, Strategy, and Execution." In *The Accountable Corporation: Corporate Social Responsibility* eds. Epstein, M. and Hanson, K., Vol. 3, 116–117. Westport, CT: Praeger Publishers.

initiatives come from all parts and levels of the organization. Moreover, while it makes sense to identify a specific business logic and rationale for each sustainability initiative, the reality is that companies often take on causes and projects that have little or no connection to their core competencies or business strategy. As such, Rangan et al. cautioned that while they were arguing for a sustainability strategy, it was not something that could or should be completely absorbed into the company's core business strategy.[6]

Companies proactively engaged in sustainability and CSR are in many ways no different than any other business: their business model needs to generate sufficient profits for the company to survive and grow (i.e., to achieve the sustainability necessary for it to be around long enough to achieve its social and/or environmental goals as well as generate income for its investors, managers, and employees). As such, sustainable companies still need to understand and apply traditional business planning techniques; however, they also need to integrate their sustainability and CSR projects and initiatives into their strategic goals and business and operating plans. Hohnen and Potts noted that there is no "one-size-fits-all" framework or method for pursuing a sustainability strategy and that each company must consider its own unique characteristics and circumstances when implementing, expanding, or modifying its sustainability programs and policies.[7] Among other things, these characteristics and circumstances include the company's overall mission and purpose, organizational culture, external environment and risk profile, operating conditions, and existing relationships with stakeholders.

Strategic planning for sustainability is far from easy or precise, if only because it requires that simultaneous consideration be given not only to economic performance and development but also to environmental protection and the social well-being of employees and other persons and groups outside of the organization. Companies and their managers are

---

[6] Rangan, K., L. Chase, and S. Karim. April 5, 2012. *Why Every Company Needs a CSR Strategy and How to Build It.* Cambridge MA: Harvard Business School Working Paper 12–088

[7] Hohnen, P., and J. Potts, ed. 2007. *Corporate Social Responsibility: An Implementation Guide for Business.* Winnipeg CAN: International Institute for Sustainable Development.

struggling to find and deploy the tools and practices that are necessary for balancing and reconciling the "triple bottom line" of profits, planet, and people. Clearly a company cannot contribute to sustainable development on a long-term basis unless it remains "in business" and this often means taking actions thought necessary for financial survival at the expense of other actions that would be environmentally or socially preferable. Even when businesses clearly understand that respecting the environment and society are necessary, it may take time for them to make the necessary changes in their operational activities and it is not always possible for companies to avoid actions that might cause short-term environmental or social harm. In those situations, however, companies need to take responsibility for their actions and remediate the damage, such as by committing to build new skills and find meaningful employment for workers laid off as part of a downsizing of operations in a specific community. Another challenge is that the empirical data that manages are used to having for their financial analysis is not as readily available for environmental and societal issues and the information that does exist is continuously changing, often technically ambiguous and subject to competing interpretations that not only make internal decision making more difficult but also muddle the regulatory environment in which businesses must operate.

Frameworks for Developing CSR and Sustainability Strategy

The path for developing and pursuing a sustainability strategy will be different for each company and will depend on its unique characteristics and circumstances; however, it is generally recognized that an effective strategy must be based on accepting the need for organizational change, a commitment to continuous improvement and strong board-level vision and oversight. Maon et al. suggested that sustainability strategy development and implementation could be considered as an organizational change process (i.e., moving from a present to a future state), or as a new way of organizing and working, with the ultimate aim being to align the organization with the dynamic demands of the business and social environment through the identification and management of stakeholder expectations.[8] Companies can consult international instruments that provide guidance and ideas for designing and implementing an effective and comprehensive CSR initiative and which have been vetted and endorsed by governments and civil society alike. Among the sources for companies to choose from are the Organisation for Economic Co-operation and Development (OECD) Guidelines for Multinational Enterprises; the International Labour Organization (ILO) Tripartite Declaration of Principles concerning Multinational Enterprises and Social Policy and Core Labour Standards; the UN Global Compact Principles; the Global Reporting Initiative Sustainability Reporting Guidelines; the International Organization for Standardization standards; the AccountAbility AA1000 Series; and the Social Accountability International SA8000 standard.[9]

In addition, there is a growing body of empirical research that has helped to build consensus on the elements of an effective framework for developing sustainability strategies including assessing current sustainability norms, standards, and practices by benchmarking against competitors and universal standards; engaging key stakeholders to raise awareness of sustainability, solicit positive participation in the sustainability strategy process, and mobilize commitment for significant organizational change; defining the specific sustainability and CSR commitments and goals and articulating a clear business case for each of them; developing an integrated strategic plan to achieve the selected sustainability goals and embed sustainability into organizational strategy; implementing the plan and the initiatives linked with sustainability and CSR; establishing internal and

---

[8] Maon, F., V. Swaen, and A. Lindgreen. 2008. *Mainstreaming the Corporate Responsibility Agenda: A Change Model Grounded in Theory and Practice.* IAG— Louvain School of Management Working Paper, (citing Dawson, P. 2003. *Understanding Organisational Change: Contemporary Experience of People at Work.* London: Sage; and George, J. and G. Jones. 1996. *Understanding and Managing Organizational Behavior.* Reading, MA: Addison-Wesley).

[9] Hohnen, P., and J. Potts, ed. 2007. *Corporate Social Responsibility: An Implementation Guide for Business.* Winnipeg CAN: International Institute for Sustainable Development, vii. Companies can also refer to guidelines prepared by local and regional governments, which presumably were prepared with reference to specific local conditions and societal values and generally benefit from participation by representatives of business, government, and labor. Id.

external communications regarding sustainability and CSR commitments and performance; evaluating, verifying, and reporting on sustainability progress; and institutionalizing the sustainability strategies and policies by embedding sustainability into corporate culture and values and aligning organizational systems to support sustainability commitments.[10]

For example, the UN Global Compact, which has been described as the largest policy initiative for businesses that are committed to aligning their operations and strategies with universally accepted principles of sustainability and CSR, has issued guidance on implementation and integration of sustainability that notes that in many ways implementing sustainability is like any other management task and called for defining sustainability goals, taking into account the issues and ideas that should have been identified during stakeholder engagement; implementing programs with a view toward achieving the goals in a timely manner; checking to make sure that the goals are being achieved through some sort of assessment or auditing process; and dealing with problems and nonconformance to goals through quality management techniques (i.e., "Plan–Do–Check–Act.").[11] Hohnen and Potts suggested an implementation framework for sustainability strategy based on the suggestions of the UN Global Compact—they referred to it as "Plan–Do–Check–Improve"—but which placed more emphasis on measuring and evaluating perfor-

---

[10] For a survey of the literature regarding frameworks about sustainability implementation, see Maon, F., V. Swaen, and A. Lindgreen. 2008. *Mainstreaming the Corporate Responsibility Agenda: A Change Model Grounded in Theory and Practice*, 56–58. IAG—Louvain School of Management Working Paper 39, (see also Figure 1.1: Proposed Integrative Framework at 62 of publication).. Frameworks discussed included Khoo, H., and K. Tan. 2002. "Using the Australian Business Excellence Framework to Achieve Sustainable Business Excellence." *Corporate Social Responsibility and Environmental Management* 9, no. 4, pp. 196–197; Werre, M. 2003. "Implementing Corporate Responsibility—The Chiquita Case." *Journal of Business Ethics* 44, nos. 2–3, p. 247; Panapanaan, V., L. Linnanen, M. Karvonen, and V. Phan. 2005. "Roadmapping Corporate Social Responsibility in Finnish Companies." *Journal of Business Ethics* 44, no. 2, 133; and Cramer, J. 2005. "Experiences with Structuring Corporate Social Responsibility in Dutch Industry." *Journal of Cleaner Production* 13, no. 6, p. 583.

[11] UN Global Compact. "Training of Trainers Course Guidance Manual." New York, NY: UN Global Compact.

mance, identifying opportunities for improvement, and engaging with stakeholders on implementing changes and improvements.[12]

The UN Global Compact also referred to an alternative systems-based approach to continuous sustainability improvement that focused more on ensuring that sustainability was integrated into organizational strategy and included four repeating stages:[13]

- Assessment: Mapping, benchmarking, and gap analysis; internal CSR surveys; nonfinancial risk assessment; stakeholder engagement; due diligence and international standards
- Strategy: Policy development; environment and climate change; community investment; supplier code of content; human resources and measurement and monitoring system
- Implementation: Senior management buy-in; staff involvement; staff training and capacity building; roll-out policies; action plans; alignment with international standards; measurement and monitoring and supply chain integration
- Communications: Internal; external; targeted; reporting and disclosure; case studies and leadership

While first published in the early 1990s, guidance from the International Institute for Sustainable Development in collaboration with Deloitte and Touche and the World Business Council for Sustainable Development remains relevant today and suggests the following steps for the process of creating a sustainability strategy and managing an enterprise based on sustainable development principles[14]:

---

[12] Hohnen, P., and J. Potts, ed. 2007. *Corporate Social Responsibility: An Implementation Guide for Business.* Winnipeg CAN: International Institute for Sustainable Development.

[13] UN Global Compact. "Training of Trainers Course Guidance Manual." New York: UN Global Compact, pp. 39–40.

[14] 1992. *Business Strategy for Sustainable Development: Leadership and Accountability for the '90s.* Winnipeg CA: International Institute for Sustainable Development, jointly with Deloitte and Touche; Business Council for Sustainable Development.

- Perform a stakeholder analysis to identify all the parties that are directly or indirectly affected by the enterprise's operations and set out the issues, concerns, and information needs of the stakeholders with respect to the organization's sustainable development activities.

- Assess the current position to determine the degree to which the company's activities line up with sustainable development principles, a process that requires evaluating the company's overall strategy, the performance of specific operations, and the effect of particular activities. This process should compare the company's current performance with the expectations of the stakeholders, review management philosophies and systems, analyze the scope of public disclosures on sustainability topics, and evaluate the ability of current information systems to produce the required data should be evaluated.

- Set sustainable development policies and objectives including articulating the basic values that the enterprise expects its employees to follow with respect to sustainable development, incorporating sustainable development objectives as an additional dimension of business strategy, setting targets for operating performance and establishing an effective external monitoring system that gathers information on new and proposed legislation; industry practices and standards, competitors' strategies, community and special interest group policies and activities. trade union concerns and technical developments (e.g., new process technologies).

- Establish a social responsibility committee of the board of directors with responsibility for setting corporate policies on sustainable development and monitoring their implementation and for dealing with issues such as health and safety, personnel policies, environmental protection, and codes of business conduct.

- Decide on a strategy taking into account the performance of other comparable organizations and with a focus on narrowing the gap between the current state of the corporation's performance and its objectives for the future. The strategy should be supported by a plan that describes how and when management expects to achieve the stated goals and the various milestones that must be reached along the way. Once the strategy and the general plan have been approved, detailed plans should be prepared indicating how the new strategy will affect operations, management systems, information systems, and reporting. Plans should be reviewed and approved by senior management following consultation with employees throughout the organization.

- Design and execute an implementation plan for the management system changes that are needed in order to achieve sustainable development objectives, a process that normally includes changing the corporate culture and employee attitudes, defining responsibilities and accountability, and establishing organizational structures, information reporting systems, and operational practices.

- Develop a supportive corporate culture to ensure that the organization and its people give their backing to the sustainable development policies. In most cases, managers will need to be retrained to change attitudes that have traditionally emphasized wealth management for the owners of the enterprise. An effort should also be made to develop a culture that emphasizes employee participation, continuous learning and improvement.

- Develop appropriate measures and standards of performance taking into account the company's sustainable development objectives and standards that have been established by government and other public agencies.

- Develop meaningful reports for internal management and stakeholders, outlining the enterprise's sustainable development objectives and comparing performance against them. Directors and senior executives use internal reports to measure performance, make decisions, and monitor the implementation of their policies and strategies. Shareholders, creditors, employees, and customers, as well as the public at large, use external corporate reports to evaluate the performance of a corporation, and to hold the directors and senior executives accountable for achieving financial, social, and environmental objectives.

- Enhance internal monitoring processes to help directors and senior managers ensure that the sustainable development policies are being implemented. Monitoring can take many forms, such as reviewing reports submitted by middle managers, touring operating sites, and observing employees performing their duties, holding regular meetings with subordinates to review reports, and to seek input on how the procedures and reporting systems might be improved, and implementing an environmental auditing program.

Guiding Principles for Driving Sustainable Business Practices

While each of the frameworks suggested previously are organized and described as an orderly continuum of steps, the reality is that developing and implementing a sustainability initiative requires that a number of activities be carried out at once. One of the first things that should be done is to getting a good idea about what the company stands for and how it operates, a process which includes document review, interviews, and observation. Concerns of internal stakeholders, such as employees, need to be identified and analyzed. At the same time, it is essential to determine who the company's most important external stakeholders are and collect information on how those stakeholders have interacted with the company and what their expectations might be with respect to the company's CSR programs. Community concerns are particularly noteworthy even though the company's relationships with other stakeholders, such as investors, customers, lenders, and supply chain partners, have a more direct impact on economic performance. Companies need to reach out to members of their communities through publications, open houses, and workshops to develop and implement ideas about how the company can be a better community member. Finally, the interests and concerns of society-in-general and regulators should be monitored on a continuous basis and companies should establish and maintain contacts with NGOs, advocates for civil society, legislators, and representatives of regulatory agencies with influence overtopics that are relevant to the company.

Becoming a sustainable business, or improving a company's current performance with respect to acting in an environmentally and socially responsible manner, requires the same sort of strategic approach as any other major corporate initiative. However, while strategic planning for sustainability has become a recognized discipline, companies and their directors and senior executives must acknowledge and seek to overcome various specific challenges the fluidity of the concepts of sustainability and CSR, ongoing debate about the allocation of responsibilities for sustainable development between governments and business, understanding and adopting new performance measures that go beyond financial results to include environmental and social dimensions, reconciling the difficult tradeoffs that often must be resolved when implementing sustainable business practices, effectively communicating with stakeholders to explain the long-term approach that is necessary for implementing sustainability and CSR, and the need to adopt new processes for decision making in the boardroom and implement internal controls that track sustainability and facilitate sustainability reporting.

Companies can overcome these challenges if they understand and follow certain best practices when determining and implementing their sustainability strategies and making investments in sustainability-related projects. First of all, companies need to align their sustainability investment activities with an overriding business mission and vision and focus those activities on projects that are both a natural fit for the company and which are perceived by the intended beneficiaries as valuable to them. In addition, companies need to set aside adequate resources to support sustainability initiatives on a long-term basis. This means integrating sustainability into the regular strategic planning and budgetary processes, rather than treating the topic as a discretionary matter that is addressed in an ad hoc fashion and maintaining sufficient funding to ensure meaningful impact. Provision should also be made for hiring and supporting a professional, dedicated management function for the sustainability initiatives, and resources planning should be flexible enough to involve employees beyond volunteerism including allowing them to participate in sustainability initiatives as part of their regular day-to-day roles. Finally, strategies, goals, and performance should also be continuously and clearly communicated throughout the company so that everyone knows the direction that has been selected and the steps that have been planned.[15]

Management of the Strategic Planning Process

In order for strategic planning to be successful and meaningful there must be active and enthusiastic participation from multiple levels of management within the firm in order to bring the most experience to the planning process and ensure that plans are made based on the full and current information about the operational activities of the firm and conditions in the marketplace. Managers at the highest level of the company—the CEO and the senior executives of all of the key functional groups and other business units—are charged with defining the strategic mission of the company and selecting and articulating the company's overriding goals and objectives. Other members of the management group operating at higher levels in the organizational structure are responsible for collecting the information that the executive group needs in order to engage in long-range planning, which usually means reports that include necessary data about operations, finances, competitive conditions, technological trends, and other important characteristics of the external environment in which the firm is operating. In addition, managers at the business unit and departmental levels should be expected to identify and implement the specific ideas, or tactical/operational plans, that are best suited to achieving the goals and objectives set at the top of the company.

Based on their extensive survey of research on dimensions of strategic planning, Sukle and Debarliev offered the following list of suggestions to managers for improving the effectiveness of their strategic planning efforts[16]:

---

[15] Adapted from "Best Practice in Corporate Social Investment." https://next-generation.co.za/best-practice-in-corporate-social-investment-csi/ (accessed May 6, 2020).

[16] Sukle, B., and S. Debarliev. 2012. "Strategic Planning Effectiveness: Comparative Analysis of the Macedonian Context." *Economic and Business Review* 14, no. 1, pp. 63–93, 88–89.

- Strategic planning should be a formalized, explicit, and ongoing organizational process with uniform planning procedures (see table below), a long-term time horizon (i.e., three or more years), and regular progress reviews.
- Organizations should select and implement an appropriate set of strategic planning techniques and ensure that managers and employees involved in the planning process have the requisite knowledge and skills to properly use the chosen techniques.
- Senior management should encourage involvement in the strategic planning process by managers at lower levels and all other employees in the organization and should take steps to increase the awareness of those persons of the importance of strategic planning and the roles that they can and should play in the planning process.
- Specific efforts should be made to identify the presence, and rectify the adverse influence, of various barriers to strategic planning implementation and effectiveness such as crises that distract attention from implementation, inadequate leadership, and direction by departmental managers, lack of overall strategic goals, and understanding of such goals by the staff, insufficiency of employee training and instruction, delays in implementation and ineffective coordination during implementation, inadequate communication, and inadequate information systems for control activities.

Skills Required for Successful Planning

Obviously a number of skills are required in order for managers to successfully conduct the planning process. For example, managers must develop the capacity to identify various alternative options and then select those options that are most suitable for the firm and its resources. This requires training in decision-making techniques, including cost–benefit analysis and computation of risk-adjusted return on investment. Many managers must also receive training and experience in planning techniques, including opportunities to actually implement their plans in their companies. Before any formal strategic planning process is implemented, the practices within the company may be rudimentary at best—managers of each department simply produce budgets and forecasts of future revenues and use this information as a basis for requesting the funds thought to be necessary to cover operating expenses. What is lacking in this approach is any detailed research on environmental factors, market trends, or the activities of competitors. Care should also be taken not to rely excessively on outside consultants in whatever planning process that may be used. Under this scenario, consultants come to the firm, interview the managers, and return with a completed plan for approval. This approach misses important opportunities for managers to be involved in the planning process and also makes it less likely that the plan will be implemented due to a lack of real emotional commitment to something that is largely the work of outsiders.

Monitoring and Evaluation of Progress Against the Plan

Regardless of the specific strategic planning processes, companies must be sure that they create adequate controls so that activities carried out in furtherance of the strategic, tactical, and operational plans can be monitored and evaluated. This serves several important purposes including making sure that the plans and their associated activities are being executed properly and on a timely basis and that adjustments can be made as necessary in order to remedy weaknesses in the original plans and/or adapt to unforeseen changes in the company's business environment. As part of the control processes the company should define short-term milestones for key strategic goals and objectives in order to be sure that the company is on the right path as it chases end results that may be several years down the road in the planning process. Similarly the controls should be used as a way to test assumptions about changes in the business environment during the planning period. For example, if the strategy is based on specific expectations regarding the pace of development of a particular technology the control processes must include a means for gauging how that technology is actually emerging. Controls are so important that firms often make significant investments in technical resources to manage the planning process and the ability to identify the need for changes in strategy and execute those changes quickly and efficiently can be an important competitive advantage in and of itself particularly when a company is competing in a dynamic market.

Measurement of Strategic Planning Effectiveness

Sukle and Debarliev surveyed the various ways that researchers have attempted to measure the "effectiveness" of strategic planning techniques and argued that "the effectiveness of strategic planning is associated with achieving formulated objectives, producing better results, or improving the organizational performance as the result of the use of strategic planning process in the companies."[17] They noted that attempts to measure strategic planning effectiveness had traditionally been limited to using financial criteria that provide a scorecard of the financial performance of the company; however, they pointed out that new approaches to assessing organizational results and performance adopted over the last few decades had expanded the notion of strategic planning effectiveness to include "many other non-financial, qualitative criteria associated with core business process, customers, employees, organizational learning and innovation and other core areas in the companies important for the overall organizational performance." These changes are welcome since strategic planning is believed to improve organizational performance in a number of complex, and often subtle, ways such as by improving coordination, communication, and control activities[18] and it is therefore necessary to factor measures of those improvements into the analysis.

Barney reported evidence of four major approaches to measuring firm performance—survival as a measure of firm performance, stakeholder approaches to performance measurement, simple accounting measures of performance, and adjusted accounting measures of performance—and noted that accounting measures were by far the most popular tools for performance measurement due, in part, to the emphasis that early trainers of strategic planning placed on the relationship between strategy

---

[17] Id. at 66.

[18] Meilich, O., and A. Marcus. 2007. "Strategic Planning and Decision-making." In *Handbook of Decision-making*, ed. Morcol, G. 433–456, 441–442. Boca Raton, FL: CRC Press.

and improving accounting measures of performance.[19] For Drucker, five measures of firm performance were considered to be necessary and sufficient for managers: market standing, innovative performance, productivity, liquidity and cash flow, and profitability.[20] Recently, however, a wide range of new tools and approaches have emerged to assist managers in developing strategy and measure the effectiveness of those strategies in positively influencing firm performance: activity-based management, value-based management, the balanced scorecard, benchmarking, and customer relationship management.[21]

Suggestions for Successful Strategy Execution

Neilson et al., a group of consultants from Booz and Company, a global management consulting firm, compiled and analyzed extraordinary amounts of data collected from more than 25,000 employees at 31 companies, and applied their own experiences in working with hundreds of other companies, to identify and rank the traits that made organizations effective at strategy execution.[22] They noted that while the first move that companies typically make when they seek to execute a new strategy is to restructure the business; in fact, there were four "fundamental building blocks" and that two of them appeared to be much more important than the others and thus should be the initial and primary focus of the strategy execution process. The building blocks, in the order of importance, were designing information flows, clarifying decision rights, aligning motivators, and making changes to the organizational structure. Neilson et al. brought the themes together by suggesting that "[e]xecution is the result

---

[19] Barney, J. 2002. *Gaining and Sustaining Competitive Advantage.* Upper Saddle River, NJ: Prentice Hall.

[20] Drucker, P. October 30, 1986. "If Earnings Aren't the Dial to Read." *Wall Street Journal.*

[21] Digman, L. 2002. *Strategic Management: Competing in a Global Information Age.* Mason, OH: Thomson Learning.

[22] Neilson, G., K. Martin, and E. Powers. June 2008. "The Secrets to Successful Strategy Execution." *Harvard Business Review*, p. 61. See also Neilson, G., and B. Pasternack. 2005. *Results: Keep What's Good, Fix What's Wrong, and Unlock Great Performance.* New York: Random House.

of thousands of decisions made every day by employees acting according to the information they have and their own self-interest."[23]

Neilson et al. argued that once companies knew and understand the issues and practices that were most important for effective strategy execution, they could implement targeted initiatives to improve their execution capabilities. Suggestions that were offered, and the "building blocks" they were intended to impact, included the following[24]:

- Focus corporate staff on supporting business-unit decision making (decision rights)
- Clarify and streamline decision-making at each operating level (decision rights)
- Focus headquarters on important strategic questions (decision rights)
- Create centers of excellence by consolidating similar functions into a single organizational unit (decision rights, information flows)
- Assign process owners to coordinate activities that span organizational functions (decision rights, information flows, and alignment of motivators)
- Establish individual performance measures (decision rights and alignment of motivators)
- Improve field-to-headquarters information flow (information flows)
- Define and distribute daily operating metrics to the field or line (information flows)
- Create cross-functional teams (information flows and aligning motivators)
- Introduce differentiating performance award (aligning motivators)
- Expand nonmonetary rewards to recognize exceptional performers (aligning motivators)
- Increase position tenure (information flows and structure)

---

[23] Id. at 62.
[24] Id. at 67.

- Institute lateral moves and rotations (information flows and structure)
- Broaden spans of control (structure)
- Decrease layers of management (structure)

CHAPTER 2

Environmental Forces and Strategic Planning

Firms and their managers do not operate in a vacuum. Instead, each of their activities, including strategic business planning, must be undertaken and understood in the context of the specific demands and requirements of the environment in which the company conducts its business activities. Among other things, the environment determines the resources that will be available to the company, including capital, human resources, raw materials, and technology. In turn, the environment also determines the success of the company as measured by the acceptance of its products and services, profitability, and satisfaction. Feedback on the outputs of the company's activities can be used to evaluate and change the mix of resources that the company must look to gather in the future from the environment. As such, for companies to achieve their goals of producing and successfully selling high-quality products and services, it is essential to establish a strong capability for environmental analysis as part of the overall strategic planning process.

There are several different ways to look at a company's environment, often referred to as the "organizational environment." For example, this environment can be thought of as consisting of two distinguishable, albeit often related, layers—the specific environment, which includes the forces (e.g., stakeholders) that can be expected to have a direct impact on the ability of the specific company to obtain the scarce resources required for the company to create value for its owners and other stakeholders; and the general environment, which includes the forces that typically will have an impact on the shape and design of all companies, including the company and other companies who may be part of the stakeholder network of the company. Companies do have some options in the way that they structure their specific environments based on the decisions made by management regarding the desired "organizational domain" of the company.[1] Probably the most important choices that a company makes will be the scope of the goods and services that the company will produce or otherwise make available and the customers that the company expects to serve, since that will largely determine the stakeholders, in addition to the customers, who will be in a position to influence the pursuit of scarce resources by the company (i.e., the specific environment)—suppliers, distributors, employees, unions, special interest groups, governmental agencies, and competitors. General environmental factors may be more difficult for companies to control, although they certainly can and must anticipate changes relating to those factors that will impact future strategic business planning. Examples of general environmental factors, which are discussed in more detail in the following, include economic forces; technological forces; political and environmental forces; and demographic, cultural, and social forces.

Another approach to analyzing strategic planning processes focuses on how managers cope with three distinct, yet related, organizational environments—the internal environment, the task environment, and the macro-environment. The "internal" environment includes its resources, capabilities, and core competencies. The resources are the firm's assets, including its personnel and the goodwill associated with its activities, and include all of the various inputs into the processes of developing, producing, and selling the company's products—capital equipment, technology, working capital, and human "know how." Resources can be tangible (i.e., financial, physical, technological and organizational) or intangible (i.e., human, innovation or reputation). Organizational capabilities are the means chosen for deploying and managing the available resources to achieve the desired goals and objectives established by the senior managers of the company. Core competencies are the resources and capabilities that afford the company a valuable and sustainable competitive advantage. While acquisition and control of resources depends on forging relationships with a wide range of stakeholders, the first challenge

---

[1] For detailed discussion of the concept of the "organizational domain" and the way that companies adapt to, and cope with, environmental forces, see Thompson, J. 1967. *Companies in Action*. New York: McGraw-Hill.

for the senior managers of the company is dealing with the key internal stakeholders—employees, directors, and outside investors. Each of these groups is a "member" of the company and will impose its own demands on the activities and conduct of management and will often have goals and objectives that differ from management and other internal stakeholders. Accordingly, management of the internal environment can be a time-consuming, and sometimes frustrating, exercise for senior managers. The process is made even more difficult by the fact that interests of members of the management group itself will often diverge. The "task" environment includes each of the stakeholder groups outside of the internal company that have an immediate impact on the company's ability to perform its primary task of meeting the requirements of its customers including the customers themselves and suppliers, lenders, labor unions, public entities (i.e., the media, governments, and special interest groups), associations (i.e., consumer groups, religious groups, etc.), and the public. In fact, the internal and task environments, taken together, are similar to the specific environment referred to earlier. The macro-environment includes the general economic, technological, sociocultural, and political forces that impact the company and each of the other stakeholders in the internal and task environments. These forces can emerge at both the regional and international levels and generally perceived as being largely out of the immediate control of most individual economic actor, particularly small- and medium-sized enterprises. The macro-environment is similar to the general environment referred to earlier.

The relationship between the "environment" and strategic business planning is not a new idea and, in fact, it is common for management to integrate some form of environmental analysis into the strategic business planning process. The usual approach was to determine where the business activities of a particular company stood along a continuum that spanned from very stable (i.e., predictable) at one extreme to very unstable (i.e., unpredictable and risky) at the other end. Companies that operated in a stable environment typically enjoyed the benefits of a loyal customer base, limited and stable competition, slow and infrequent changes in the technology underlying their basic products and services, and a predictable body of laws and regulations. Ironically, the environment for U.S. car manufacturers, and many manufacturers of consumer goods, could be characterized as stable for most of the first part of the twentieth century and the same can be said for service industries such as banking and securities. In contrast, companies that entered new and uncharted fields such as computers and software, telecommunications, and biotechnology found themselves in unstable and rapid changing environments that were difficult to navigate and predict. Certainly, many well-known companies—IBM, Microsoft, Hewlett Packard, Intel, and Genentech—overcame the challenges of an unstable environment to become some of the major economic players in recent years; however, many more companies with promising business ideas failed, at least in part, because of their inability to navigate the choppy waters of the modern global business environment.

Obviously, if they had their choice the managers of any new business would choose a stable business environment provided that they could reasonably expect to realize a sufficient return on the company's investment in resources to meet or exceed the expectations of their stakeholders. Unfortunately, there is now little doubt that more and more businesses, including small businesses looking to operate in a limited market niche, must deal with and attempt to manage an unstable business environment. The developments behind this change are well documented and publicized—improvements in information processing, telecommunications, and transportation; rapid changes in technology; growth and development of markets in foreign countries; and growing discernment in consumer tastes that have caused customer loyalty to almost disappear. The Internet, for example, has created thousands of potential niche markets and enabled a number of new strategies for creating customer relationships. As a result, companies are now compelled to be part of an international marketplace in which competition can emerge suddenly from anywhere in the world and the search for the resources that are necessary for competitive advantage—raw materials, technology, low-cost manufacturing—must be conducted globally. The dramatic, and likely permanent, turn toward instability in the business environment places makes strategic business planning an even higher priority for companies of all sizes.

Specific Environment

Two of the most important goals of the business planning process for any company are defining the organizational domain of the company and devising and executing strategies to continuously expand that domain in a way that creates additional value for the company's key stakeholders. The organizational domain consists of a number of different elements and constituencies. In addition to the products and services that the company products or otherwise makes available for sale, the organizational domain includes various stakeholders with a vested interest in the inputs and outputs of the business and in the way that the business operations— customers, suppliers, distributors, and employees as well as governmental agencies, unions, communities, special interest groups, and other firms competing with the company in the same markets. These stakeholders, taken together, define the "specific environment" in which the company must operate, preferably in a deliberate and strategic manner.

The specific environment is sometimes broken down into various subcategories. For example, it may be useful to distinguish between the "input" environment, which includes the markets where the company seeks the scarce resources that will be used to create the company's products and services (e.g., raw materials, technology, skilled human resources, working capital); and the "output" environment, which includes the markets into which the company proposed to distribute its products and services (i.e., customers). Still another approach, as previously noted,, focuses on how managers deal with internal and task environments. The "internal" environment includes employees, outside investors, and the members of the board of directors if the company is organized in the corporate form. The "task" environment includes each of the stakeholder groups outside of the internal company that have an immediate impact on the company's ability to perform its primary task of meeting the requirements of its customers including the customers themselves and suppliers, lenders, labor unions, public entities (i.e., the media, governments, and special interest groups), associations (i.e., consumer groups, religious groups, etc.), and the public.

In any event, all of the activities associated with the various segments of the company's specific environment (e.g., establishing, coordinating, and controlling stakeholder relationships) will create transaction costs for the company and the senior management of the company must develop strategies to manage and influence these environmental factors in a way that allows the company to maximize its ability to successfully identify, obtain, and maintain the resources necessary to launch the company and continuously grow its business and eventually expand its organizational domain. The issues in this area are crucial since every company is dependent on the relative stability of its specific environment and each of the stakeholders has the ability to exert significant influence on the company, its managers, and other stakeholders to act in certain ways.

Products, Services, and Customers

Companies and their managers must be adept at several different types of analytical and strategic tools in order to successfully define their organizational domain and the relevant specific environmental factors. For example, one of the first steps in establishing the organizational domain is determining the initial products and/or services of the company and identifying the first group of potential customers that the company intends to serve offering those products and/or services. The choice of products and services depends on a number of factors, most notably the background and technical and business skills of the founders of the company. It is essential, however, to remember that any product or service, regardless of its novelty or assumed utility, will only be valuable to the company if it attracts the essential scarce resource—a loyal customer base that can be grown to expand the company's organizational domain. Accordingly, when developing the company's strategy and accompanying business plan, the management team must zealously pursue information about the company's target customer base and the steps that must be taken in order to satisfy customer needs. In addition, the business plans for companies that are just starting out and seeking to attain rapid growth must anticipate in advance introduction of follow-on products and services and expansion of the customer base beyond the initial group.

For a long time, strategic planning with respect to development and commercialization of products and services focused primarily on features, pricing and the iconic "five Ps" of the marketing mix (i.e., product, price, promotion, place, and people); however, companies must now plan and execute their strategies in a manner that adequately and effectively addresses various consumer issues relating to social responsibility including, among other things, fair marketing practices (i.e., using fair, transparent, and helpful marketing information and contractual processes); protection of consumers' health and safety (e.g., minimizing risks from the use of products and services, through design, testing, manufacture, distribution, information provision, support services, and withdrawal and recall procedures); sustainable consumption (e.g., reducing waste by minimizing packing material and, if appropriate, offering recycling and disposal services; and eliminating or minimizing negative health and environmental impacts of products and services, such as noise or waste); consumer service, support, and complaint and dispute resolution; consumer data and privacy protection; access to essential products and services; addressing the informational and other needs of vulnerable and disadvantaged consumers (e.g., those with limited vision or hearing, or poor reading ability); and promotion of education and awareness.[2]

Strategic planning for socially responsible companies should include plans and resources for the development and implementation of the following socially responsible practices regarding the legitimate needs of consumers described in the UN Guidelines for Consumer Protection[3]:

---

[2] ISO 26000 Guidance on Social Responsibility (Geneva: International Organization for Standardization, 2010), 52. For further discussion, see Gutterman, A. 2019. *Responsible Business: A Guide to Corporate Social Responsibility for Sustainable Entrepreneurs.* Oakland CA: Sustainable Entrepreneurship Project. available: www.seproject.org.

[3] Additional principles laid out in the UN Guidelines that are relevant to socially responsible practices relating to consumers include respect for the right to privacy, the precautionary approach (i.e., where there are threats of serious or irreversible damage to the environment or human health, lack of full scientific certainty should not be used as a reason for postponing cost-effective measures to prevent environmental degradation or damage to human health) and promotion of gender equality and empowerment of women and prevention of the perpetuation of gender stereotypes. Id. at 53–54.

- *Safety*: The right of access to nonhazardous products and protection of consumers from hazards to their health and safety stemming from production processes, products and services
- *Being Informed*: Access of consumers to adequate information to enable them to make informed choices according to individual wishes and needs and to be protected against dishonest or misleading advertising or labeling
- *Making Choices*: The promotion and protection of the economic interests of consumers, including the ability to select from a range of products and services, offered at competitive prices with an assurance of satisfactory quality
- *Being Heard*: Freedom to form consumer and other relevant groups or organizations and the opportunity of such organizations to present their views in decision-making processes affecting them, especially in the making and execution of government policy, and in the development of products and services
- *Redress*: Availability of effective consumer redress, in particular in the form of fair settlement of just claims, including compensation for misrepresentation, badly made products, or unsatisfactory services
- *Education*: Consumer education, including education on the environmental, social and economic impacts of consumer choice, enables consumers to make informed, independent choices about products and services while being aware of their rights and responsibilities and how to act on them
- *Healthy Environment*: Contributing to creation and maintenance of an environment that is not threatening to the well-being of present and future generations by ensuring that products and services are economically, socially, and environmentally sustainable
- *Promotion of Universal Design*: Design of products and environments to be usable by all people, to the greatest extent possible, without the need for adaptation or specialized design[4]

---

[4] There are seven principles to universal design: equitable use, flexibility in use, simple and intuitive use, perceptible information, tolerance for error, low physical effort and size and space for approach and use. Id. at 54.

Value Chain Partners: Suppliers and Distributors

Another important aspect of building the organizational domain is accessing certain key inputs necessary for development and commercialization of the chosen products and/or services. For example, companies must decide on the best strategies for obtaining necessary raw materials and technologies. While it may be possible to create these inputs internally, companies often turn to external sources. All companies, regardless of their size, are dependent in some way on the acquisition and use of products and services from suppliers. Among other things, the firm may look to an outside vendor for raw materials, equipment, consulting services, or manufacturing. As such, one of the keys to success for any firm is its ability to consistently locate and select the best suppliers offering the required products and services at the right prices, quality, location, and time. This issue has become even more important as globalization and increased competitiveness in the marketplace has created significant pressures on managers to streamline their supply chains. As customer demand higher levels of quality, and shorter delivery times, businesses have become much more reliant on their supplier relationships.

A variety of supplier strategies are now in use, including the use of long-term contracts with supplier to ensure availability of needed products and even backward integration through acquisition of control of key suppliers. Companies are also making use of breakthroughs in information technology and communications as the basis for "just-in-time" procurement strategies, rather than stockpiling supplies in inventory. In any event, companies must carefully evaluate the supply function to identify the optimal sources of supply and establish supply relationships that suit the requirements of the company with respect to quality and reliability, pricing and terms of payment, and delivery. Moreover, these relationships must be carefully nurtured and managed as key suppliers inevitably become fixtures within the company's organizational domain.

While supplier relationships can be used to leverage a company's own resources and accelerate expansion of the underlying business, the growing dependence on suppliers has created new challenges for the strategic planning process. Companies must now be mindful of, and plan for, "supply chain management," which often becomes a centerpiece of the

company's CSR strategies and programs. Companies have come to understand that it will no longer be acceptable to select value chain partners
based solely on traditional methods such as "lowest cost" and that consideration must be given to both the positive and negative environmental and social consequences of offering business to a particular partner.
Supply chain management is a challenging undertaking since, although
leverage from a business relationship with a partner can be a strong influence on the partner's behavior, it is ultimately up to the partner to determine its own level of legal and regulatory compliance and how its actions
impact the environment and society.

In order to make the best effort to fulfill its CSR-related responsibilities
with respect to supply chain management, companies must have in place
a rigorous program for assessing their significant suppliers and contractors
with respect to important CSR subjects such as human rights, health and
safety, anticorruption, and environmental practices. The goal of the assessment is to make a reasonable determination as to whether or not suppliers
and contractors are adhering to adequate social and environmental standards, in compliance with the law, international standards and best CSR
practice. The form and rigor of the assessment process will vary depending
on the scope of the relationship, the proximity of the supplier or contractor
to the company's facilities, and the company's available resources. Companies may rely on external social auditing companies to assess their suppliers
and/or their own internal teams that generate questionnaires for suppliers
and contractors and periodically visit the facilities of suppliers and contractors to conduct inspections and interviews in order to verify the responses
in the questionnaires. There are risks of CSR problems with every supplier
or contractor and a problem with even a small supplier can become a huge
reputational headache for a company; however, few companies have the
resources to go beyond monitoring their first tier suppliers and contractors.[5]

---

[5] CSR Self-Assessment Handbook for Companies (Vilnius, Lithuania: UAB "Baltijos
kopija" (Financed by the European Union and United Nations Development Programme), 2010), 68. Companies may often have to "sub-contract" the CSR monitoring and assessment process to first tier suppliers and contractors by requiring them
to assess their own supply chains and report to the company regarding any material
compliance issues and the steps taken to address those issues.

The toolkit for supply chain management not only includes a formal policy and related processes on engagement with supply chain partners, which should be approved by the board of directors and reviewed no less than annually by the board or a committee of the board created as the primary oversight body for CSR but also codes of conduct for suppliers, assessment tools reflecting analysis of underlying causes of violations, metrics on human rights and anticorruption practices at business partners, corrective action plans, evidence of remediation, evidence of using the collected information to inform an improved supply chain management policy and model sourcing contracts with mandatory provisions relating to CSR matters such as human rights (particularly for suppliers with operations in jurisdictions with a reputation for shortcomings in protections of human rights by the state and/or business enterprises) and environmentally sound practices. Particularly with larger suppliers, the supply chain management process should focus attention on the labor practices of the supplier using criteria similar to that which applies to the company own operations, as subsequently discussed.

Companies must also enter into acceptable arrangements with outside dealers and distributors to make the products and services available for sale to customers and must also establish relationships with banks and other financial institutions, as well as investors, in order to obtain working capital on acceptable terms and conditions. While we discuss elements of the organizational domain separately, there are obvious connections that will require managers to go back and forth between various issues. For example, before settling on the design elements and pricing characteristics of a new product or service the company must be sure that its suppliers can deliver inputs (i.e., components and/or finished goods) with the desired features and at an acceptable cost level. Similarly, the company's selection of a customer base and customer satisfaction strategy must be aligned with the resources of the company's distribution network.

Labor Practices

With respect to employees, companies must be able to recruit and retain skilled workers, including managers and technical specialists, who can build and maintain a competitive advantage for the company while still allowing the company to operate at a competitive level with respect to salaries and the costs of employee benefits. In order to effectively manage employees, managers must be mindful of the motivations and goals of the workers and the organizational culture. In most parts of the world, employees rely on their positions within the firm to earn a wage and the compensation they receive from their employers is generally their primary source of income and means of livelihood. In many cases, the income received by workers is also used to support their extended family. However, motivating workers is not simply a matter of compensation and managers must learn to understand the basic individual needs of employees, which will vary depending on the circumstances and change continuously as time goes by and employees go through different stages of their careers, and then must create and implement programs that align the needs of employees with the strategic goals and objectives of the company. This process, challenging enough in industrialized countries, is even more difficult in developing countries because workers in many of those countries remain loyal to traditional affiliations, such as religious and ethnic ties. As a result, managers must be able to appreciate and understand how these affiliations create important informal networks within the company. In addition, managers must strive to create a workplace culture that accommodates and respects local norms and values while promoting the effective use of new productivity tools and practices.

Labor unions, through the collective bargaining process, can have a significant impact of working conditions, wages, hours, and other issues that are important in determining the specific environment of the company. If labor unions are involved the company must be prepared to engage in vigorous, often heated, negotiations regarding wages, benefits and protection for union workers against reductions in force. Labor unions in developing countries are often part of a broad network of groups that can exert significant political leverage at national and regional levels. In addition to collective bargaining negotiations, representatives from labor unions in foreign countries may become more involved in internal matters through service of company committees, including those responsible for hiring and promotion decisions.

The skills of a company's labor force—employees and contractors— and the costs associated with recruitment and retention are obviously key factors for the company's potential competitive advantage; however, strategies relating to human capital must be conceptualized broadly to include a wide range of "labor practices" including the recruitment and promotion of workers; disciplinary and grievance procedures; the transfer and relocation of workers; termination of employment; training and skills development; health, safety and industrial hygiene; any policy or practice affecting conditions of work, in particular working time and remuneration; and the recognition of worker organizations and representation and participation of both worker and employer organizations in collective bargaining, social dialogue and tripartite consultation to address social issues related to employment. In its Section 6.4.1.2, ISO 26000 argues that the creation of jobs, as well as the wages and other compensation paid for work performed, are among an organization's most important economic and social contributions.[6] As such, it is not surprising that companies have formalized their planning in this area through the creation of strategic human capital plans.

The issues and prospective actions relative to labor practices are obviously broad and far-ranging and companies are advised to create a formal action plan regarding labor and human resources and evaluate it on a regular basis. A simple structure for such a plan would include goals and targets for improvement; actions necessary for improvement; responsibilities for each action and the relative priorities of the various actions; timelines; and procedures for monitoring, evaluation and communication of progress. Within this structure, the content of the plan should cover topics such as practices on engagement with employee representatives in a fair way for both parties; practices on assurance of nondiscrimination and gender equality; health and safety preventive actions; practices on mitigation of job losses; practices on establishment of compensation levels and how people can earn more (e.g., bonuses, promotions etc.); practices on establishment of fair conditions of work, beyond what is legally required; benefits in addition to those stipulated by law provided to workers of

---

[6] Section 6.4.2.1 of ISO 26000 references various sources of fundamental principles relating to labor practices and social responsibility including the ILO's 1944 Declaration of Philadelphia, the Universal Declaration of Human Rights and the International Covenant on Economic, Social and Cultural Rights.

all contract types (e.g., full-time, part-time, contract, seasonal, etc.), and practices on grievance procedures and disciplinary action. Development of the action plan should be done through a participative process of engagement that seeks out input from senior management and employees. A senior staff member should be responsible for collecting the information and driving the completion of the plan, which should be formally approved by the board of directors. Most importantly, the plan should be a living document that is taken seriously, not just another policy or aspirational statement that is posed on the website and then forgotten.[7]

Regulators

Companies deal with applicable laws and regulations by developing compliance programs and ensuring that their manufacturing activities and their workplace environment meets or exceeds the basic requirements established by labor, health, and safety laws. It is well known that business regulation in the United States is extensive in scope and touches upon on all aspects of the employment relationship—recruiting, compensation, evaluation, and discipline. In many cases the products and services developed and offered by technology-based companies must be vetted and approved by regulatory agencies (e.g., the federal Food and Drug Administration in the case of pharmaceutical products) and companies in that situation must be sure they understand and adhere to specific regulatory guidelines and concepts of best practices in the relevant industry. In developing countries the same role is played by medical and pharmacy boards, which regulate the development and local sale of medicines and other pharmaceutical products. Regulation can also come in the form of oversight by sectoral associations, such as accounting boards and associations, which regulate financial reporting practices and marketing associations.

---

[7] CSR Self-Assessment Handbook for Companies (Vilnius, Lithuania: UAB "Baltijos kopija" (Financed by the European Union and United Nations Development Programme), 2010), 40–41.

Communities

Social responsibility requires that companies recognize their roles and obligations as citizens of the communities in which they operate. While it is common for "society" to be identified as an organizational stakeholder, communities are the place in which companies can make a difference in some small, yet meaningful way, on improving environmental and social conditions. Focusing on the community level allows a company to set meaningful targets and implement programs that fit its specific scale of operations and which can provide meaningful value to the company and its stakeholders. Communities find their way into strategic planning through "community involvement and development," which includes integrating actions that benefit communities (e.g., job creation, skill development, wealth and income creation and provision of health, welfare and other services) into the company's core business model.[8]

The issues for businesses relating to community involvement and development identified in ISO 26000 include community involvement and respecting the laws and practices of the community; social investment (i.e., building infrastructure and improving social aspects of community life); employment creation (i.e., making decisions to maximize local employment opportunities); technology development (i.e., engaging in partnerships with local organizations and facilitating diffusion of technology into the community to contribute to economic development); wealth and income (i.e., use natural resources in a sustainable way that helps to alleviate poverty, give preference to local suppliers, and fulfill tax responsibilities); education and culture (i.e., support education at all levels and promote cultural activities); health (i.e., promote good health, raise awareness about diseases, and support access to essential health care

---

[8] According to ISO 26000, the term "community" in the relevant clause refers to residential or other social settlements located in a geographic area that is in physical proximity to an organization's sites or within an organization's areas of impact; however, ISO 26000 notes that the area and the community members affected by an organization's impacts will depend upon the context and especially upon the size and nature of those impacts and also points out that the term community can be understood to mean a group of people having particular characteristics in common, for instance a "virtual" community concerned with a particular issue. Id. at 61.

services); and responsible investment (i.e., incorporate economic, social, environmental, and governance dimensions into investment decisions along with traditional financial dimensions).[9] Each of these topics can and must be approached strategically. For example, when considering a community investment project, companies must take into account factors such as impact, sustainability, factors for success, implementation partners, timeline, business case, budget, local engagement, and ownership and relationship to operational activities.[10]

Special Interest Groups

Companies must also be mindful of special interest groups such as social activists dedicated to environmental protection, consumer rights, and advancement of women and/or ethnic groups. For example, consumer advocates may apply pressure on companies to refrain from engaging in certain practices such as importing raw materials from specific foreign countries (i.e., countries with a reputation for failure to adopt and/or enforce laws and regulations pertaining to protection of basic human rights or the environment) or utilizing manufacturing processes that might reduce the safety or quality of the company's products. At a minimum, activists may increase the level of scrutiny of the manner in which firms conduct their businesses. Increasingly, social activism has led to the adoption of laws and regulations that clearly impact the manner in which firms must operate. This phenomenon has even been spreading to developing countries as they begin to realize the importance of protecting their vast natural resources and create property rights to provide real incentives for conservation and reduction of pollution. Consumer protection laws are being adopted in developing countries to protect the health and safety of users and encourage companies to use high-quality manufacturing and quality assurance practices. Some developing countries are also beginning

---

[9] *Handbook for Implementers of ISO 26000, Global Guidance Standard on Social Responsibility by Small and Medium Sized Businesses* (Middlebury VT: ECOLOGIA, 2011), 32–33.

[10] *Corporate Social Responsibility Processes and Practices Manual: Operating Guidelines* (Africa Oil Kenya B.V., July 2015).

to cast aside traditional male-oriented values in favor of new guidelines to increase employment opportunities for women.

Competitors

Finally, it should not be forgotten that competitors are also part of the organizational domain designed by a company. The selection of products and services and customer markets, as well as the identification of the human and technological resources necessary for the business to operate, will determine which firms the company will need to compete with in order to gain access to, and control over, scarce resources including customers, suppliers, distributors, talented workers, and capital. While it used to be that competition generally came from domestic firms it is now the rule, rather than the exception, that companies can expect challenges from U.S. firms and from companies based overseas. It is well known that many emerging companies are launched "under the radar" with a focus on niche markets that are too small or unorganized to garner interest from established incumbents. In this way the new company can reduce and manage the impact of competition on its activities. Companies can also attempt to manage competition by tying up scarce resources, such as by entering into exclusive supply arrangements with key vendors for raw materials. Another way to deal with competitors is to forge alliances, either directly with a competitor or with other small firms, to create a critical mass of resources that can compete with larger firms on the basis of economies of scale.

Stakeholder Engagement Strategies

Effective and strategic engagement with each of the stakeholders described earlier should be considered essential to proper execution of a company's strategic plan. Stakeholders are important partners in, and catalysts for, the organizational change that is generally the focus and purpose of strategic planning. As such, stakeholder engagement strategies must be developed that take into account the level of interest and scope of influence of each of the stakeholder groups in a particular strategic initiative and the goals that stakeholders would like to see the company to pursue with respect to its strategic planning process. While the company is ultimately responsible for what goes into its strategic plan and how the plan is executed, stakeholder input should be sought and taken seriously and the company should be prepared to commit to continuous dialogue and reporting (i.e., transparency) as a means for building and maintaining strong long-term relationships with each of its key stakeholders and accepting accountability for its actions and how they affect the world in which the company operates. When vetting a particular project or initiative, traditional financial targets, such as increasing shareholder value, should not be the sole criteria. In addition, assessment and analysis should include the projected positive and negative impact of the project and initiative on the overall well-being of all stakeholders. At the same time, it is also fair and necessary to identify specific responsibilities that stakeholders might have with respect to executing a program or initiative that will have value to them if it successful.[11]

For example, since there are so many ways that a company can fulfill its social responsibilities to the communities in which it operates, it is important to take a strategic approach to community engagement and involvement, which means creating a "community engagement action plan" that includes goals/targets for improvement, the actions necessary for meeting targets, responsibilities for each action and priorities of actions, timelines and procedures for monitoring, and evaluation and communication of progress. The content of the plan would be specific to the goals selected by the company. Engagement with community stakeholders should certainly be covered. For example, it should be common practice for company representatives to consult with community members prior to acquiring property and/or making material changes in business operations. Other projects and activities might include participation in CSR industry groups, employee volunteer programs, and other philanthropic activities and apprenticeship programs for community members to improve their job-related skills. Community engagement is an essential

---

[11] An important tool for effective stakeholder engagement is the latest version of the AA1000 AccountAbility Stakeholder Engagement Standard, which has become the most widely applied global stakeholder engagement standard, supporting organizations to assess, design, implement, and communicate an integrated approach to stakeholder engagement.

and crucial part of becoming and remaining a socially responsible business and companies should document and report on their engagement activities and efforts to resolve disputes that may arise with groups within the community.[12]

General Environmental Factors

Each company, regardless of its specific business activities and related organizational domain, must also operate and survive within a broad general environment that includes forces that will eventually impact the ability of every company within that environment to obtain the resources required for their activities. The strategic business plan for the company should take into account relevant trends that can be expected to have a major impact on the company's activities over the planning period. Examples of issues to consider include demographic changes, economic policies and conditions, technological developments, the emergence of new competitors, regulatory changes, and the activities of special interest groups. The following is a brief description of some of the more important and common general environmental forces.

Economic Forces

These forces might include interest rates, exchanges rates, wage levels, GDP, per capita income, unemployment rates, and other indicators of the general health and condition of the economy have a direct and significant impact on the demand for the products and services of companies and the prices that must be paid in order for companies to obtain necessary resources (e.g., raw materials and personnel). Differences between countries with respect to certain of these key economic indicators can have a dramatic impact on choices that companies make

---

[12] *CSR Self-Assessment Handbook for Companies* (Vilnius, Lithuania: UAB "Baltijos kopija" (Financed by the European Union and United Nations Development Programme), 2010), 55.

when designing their organizational domains. For example, it is now common for U.S. companies of all sizes to outsource manufacturing and other activities to foreign countries where the relative costs of labor and/or raw materials are lower and, in fact, outsourcing to reduce costs has become an essential strategy for remaining competitive in global marketplaces.

Technological Forces

These might include development of new technologies that will ultimately lead to new products and services, more efficient production techniques, and new methods for accelerating communications and exchange of data will always have a significant and often sudden impact on how companies operate. A complicating factor for U.S. companies is that more and more new technologies are being developed outside of the United States and U.S. companies must learn how to identify breakthroughs in foreign markets and transfer them into their own companies so that they can be used to remain competitive.

Political and Environmental Forces

These might include laws and regulations, politically driven governmental policies, and pressure from special interest groups, which may impact how companies will need to interact with governmental agencies. A simple example is how companies have been forced to address concerns raised by environmental interest groups regarding how certain products may adversely affect the environment. In many cases, companies have been forced to invest significant amounts in redesigning products or packaging to reduce pollution or solid waste and this has typically required modifications in the relationships that these companies have with key stakeholders such as customers and suppliers. In some instances, the need to respond to special interest groups has caused companies to join forces, albeit temporarily, with competitors in an effort to counterbalance the resources that the interest groups might be using to influence public policymakers. Political forces are obviously relevant to companies as they expand globally since foreign countries may regulate inbound foreign investment and/or establish and enforce import and export controls in order to manage the impact of foreign investment on their local economies.

Demographic, Cultural, and Social Forces

These might include age, level of education, customs and values, lifestyle, and religious beliefs within a particular country or geographic territory and will determine the business methods and practices in the country or territory and impact how a company must relate to key stakeholders—customers, employees, suppliers, distributors, and regulators—in those countries and territories. These forces will determine what products and services might be most popular in a particular country and the attitudes of customers regarding products and services that are imported from the United States and other foreign countries. With respect to how business is conducted in foreign countries, U.S. companies must be mindful of how local culture, customs, and values shape attitudes toward business practices that might be considered corrupt in the United States yet are seen as acceptable in the foreign country. Culture may also impact how local companies comply with financial reporting requirements and will also influence the role that local labor unions play in relations between managers and employees.

While the general environmental forces described previously will ultimately impact every element of a company's specific environment, they are particularly relevant to the selection of products and services and the target customer base. Since emerging companies are typically launched to create and exploit some type of technology-based competitive advantage their business models are particularly sensitive to technological forces. As a result, it is not surprising to see that emerging companies tend to make technology-related activities a priority in the business planning process and are more likely to dedicate resources to technology planning and forecasting at a very early stage of the company's development. Economic, demographic, and cultural forces are also important factors for emerging companies looking to launch new products and services in dynamic industries such as communications and entertainment. Finally, if the founders believe that a potential product or service will have a global market, they must carefully consider cultural and political factors in key foreign markets before the initial design of the product or service is completed to ensure that it can be easily and efficiently rolled out with minimal additional expense and effort to localize the product or service for successful entry in foreign markets.

While general economic forces present significant challenges for firms primarily active in industrialized countries, managers of companies in developing countries face an almost overwhelming task in coping with the turbulent economic and political forces that are continually in play in their domestic markets. Among other things, managers in developing countries must deal with rapid and frequent fluctuations in interest rates and inflation, devaluation of national currencies, constantly changing regulatory and industrial policies, and unstable markets and prices for raw materials and other inputs. An area of particular concern is the political environment, which can impact business conditions in developing countries in several important ways:

- The level of political stability in the country has a substantial impact on the climate in which managers must operate and directly impacts the new business opportunities that might be available to local firms. Unfortunately, political conditions in many developing countries remain unstable, and are often defined by lengthy periods of civil unrest and struggles among various interest groups. The increased political risk often causes foreign investors to look elsewhere for markets and business relationships.
- The government establishes the economic and industrial policies, laws and regulations, and incentive programs that can promote or restrict business activities. For example, government registration requirements for business licenses, export activities, and import of raw materials can be quite costly and time-consuming. On the other hand, the government may provide needed funding for product development and tax deferrals and exemptions to encourage export activities. The impact of the government's legal authority extends to all parts of the business company: labor laws influence how the company operates its human resources function; consumer protection and competition laws must be

taken into account in product development and marketing; and the finance department must comply with accounting rules and financial disclosure requirements.

- Even in industrialized countries, governments remain significant consumers of products and services generated in the private sector. In fact, for many companies that are engaged in the development and manufacture of military equipment, the government is their primary, if not sole, market. As such, managers must learn to evaluate government procurement offices in the same way as any other customer and, if appropriate, develop the necessary expertise to understand the detailed procedures for bidding on government contracts.

- While privatization has become an important part of industrial policy in many developing countries, a substantial number of state-owned firms remain in existence. As such, the government, through these "parastatals," may be directly involved in market activities and provide substantial competition to private sector firms.

International and regional economic and political factors are becoming increasingly important for firms in industrialized and developing countries. Rapid improvements in technology and communications have created global marketplaces where goods can be sold quickly and easily. The World Trade Organization, the latest in a series of efforts to build a permanent and viable multilateral trade institution, has created additional rules and regulations for international trade and market access that supersede the domestic policies of member nations. Finally, the rise of regional trade companies throughout the world, including the industrialized areas of North America and Europe, promises to have a significant impact on marketing strategies.

Internationalization is already having several significant effects on the day-to-day activities and concerns of managers in the developing countries. First of all, firms may initially suffer from the loss of preferences previously afforded to developing countries under prior treaties and conventions. Second, companies in developing countries are also likely to experience increased competition in their home markets as tariffs are liberalized around the world and their governments are forced to discontinue protectionist policies. Third, the required skill base for managers must evolve to include the tools necessary for analyzing and understanding foreign markets, each of which have their own unique set of environmental factors.

CHAPTER 3

Conducting a CSR Assessment

While frameworks and suggestions for implementation of corporate social responsibility (CSR) do vary, there is almost no controversy that in order to make informed decisions about the content of a new CSR initiative, or changes to an existing program, the board of directors and members of the senior management team must engage in a rigorous assessment process in order to obtain an accurate picture of the current state of the company's efforts and activities with respect to economic, environmental, and social responsibility. The assessment process will rely on a variety of tools and actions including internal surveys, stakeholder engagement, and reviews of publicly available data for peer organizations (e.g., corporate websites, annual reports, and CSR reports). Assessments can be done using internal resources or organizations can turn to outside consultants for assistance. In either case, reference can be made to one or more of the formal procedures that have been developed to assess the level of an organization's responsibility such as SA8000, AA 1000, and ISO 26000. There is no universal template for conducting a CSR assessment, and how information is collected depends on organization-specific factors such as available resources, products, and services and the legal and other external environment; however, key elements of an effective assessment include assembling a skilled and experienced working group, developing a working definition of CSR; identifying legal requirements; reviewing corporate documents, processes and activities; identifying and engaging key stakeholders through interviews, surveys, and observation; identifying and measuring economic, social, and environmental impacts; and identifying and prioritizing key CSR activities. Assessment should be seen as a continuous process, which means information and results should be collected and carefully inventoried in order to provide a foundation for new inquiries in subsequent planning periods.

Assembling a CSR Leadership Team

CSR is like any other important management initiative and requires leadership from the top of the organization, starting with the board of directors, and active support and participation from key personnel at all other levels within the company. Hohnen and Potts recommended that organizations convene a CSR leadership team during the assessment phase to plan and coordinate all of the activities required for the assessment to fulfill its objectives and to set the stage for the CSR implementation and integration work that will follow the initial assessment. The team should initially be composed of representatives from the board of directors and senior management or owners as well as representatives from each of the business units (functional, geographic, and product-based) within the company who are either affected by or involved in CSR issues and projects. Other members of the team should include senior personnel and frontline personnel from human resources, environmental services, health and safety, community relations, legal affairs, finance, marketing, and communications.[1] Having frontline personnel on the team from the beginning is important because the success of many of the activities depends on the performance of employees who deal with customers and other business partners on a day-to-day business and are actively involved in the design and manufacturing of the company's products. As the CSR initiative is implemented the composition of the leadership team may change as it becomes clearer what types of skill are needed for the initiative to be successful. Each member of the team should be enthusiastic about CSR and knowledgeable about some aspect of the CSR strategy. Directors and senior executives on the team, as well as all the other members, should be expected to be champions and ambassadors of CSR throughout the organization and in communication with the company's stakeholders.

---

[1] Hohnen, P., and J. Potts, ed. 2007. *Corporate Social Responsibility: An Implementation Guide for Business*, 23. Winnipeg CAN: International Institute for Sustainable Development.

The creation and selection of the leadership team should be overseen and approved by the board of directors and the board should require regular reports on the progress of the team including any recommendations for high-level decisions that should be made by the board with respect to the company's CSR initiatives. As time goes by, changes might be made to the compensation arrangements for certain members of the leadership team, particularly senior executives, in order to align their financial rewards and incentives with achievement of specific performance goals relating to environmental and social responsibility. For example, PepsiCo established individual performance objectives for its senior leaders on a range of areas such as driving and enhancing sustainable innovation, improving operational efficiencies, increasing customer satisfaction, and managing and developing a diverse and talented workforce. The leadership team also becomes the nurturing ground for what will eventually become more formal and permanent organizational structures for the company's sustainability activities. During the assessment process, notes should be taken and cataloged regarding the appropriate ways to organize the company's CSR initiatives and leverage all of the data that is being collected during the assessment. Among other things, of the members of the leadership team selected to represent specific functions, geographic areas, or product lines can focus on the best way to integrate CSR into their business groups including internal processes (e.g., sustainability officers and departments) and liaison relationships with other groups throughout the organization.

The leadership team should be more than just a collection of noteworthy personalities (and persons with lofty titles) from throughout the organization. Members of the team should expect to devote significant time and effort to the entire CSR initiative, typically displacing a good deal of the activities that they had normally been engaged with before joining the team. While the first stage of the team's responsibilities will be focused on the assessment process, team members will eventually be heavily involved in discussions and decisions relating to the company's actual CSR strategies and the organizational resources that will be set aside for CSR programs. Team members will become the primary liaisons to key internal and external stakeholders, starting with the board of directors and then moving on to include investors, employees, suppliers and other business partners, government officials, and representatives of consumer groups and social activists interested in the company's CSR activities. While the team must eventually speak with essentially a single voice, having a diverse range of perspectives is important during the assessment and planning process in order to ensure that all viewpoints regarding the relationship between the company and CSR are heard and taken into account when make strategy decisions. The team should settle on a reasonable decision-making process during its initial meetings, a process that should be flexible enough to facilitate consensus building yet strict enough to make decisions final once sufficient information has been collected and an appropriate debate has occurred.

Developing a Working Definition of CSR

In order for the assessment to proceed efficiently toward the ultimate goal of developing and implementing a CSR strategy, the leadership team should define exactly what the term CSR means for the company. The team should work with people from all levels of the organizational hierarchy of the company to develop a working definition, a process that not only ensures that all relevant issues and stakeholders will be incorporated into the definition but also builds a foundation for broad support of the initiative throughout the organization. The definition is usually somewhat general and refers to the overall goals and objectives of the company, the company's stakeholders, key elements of CSR, and the key values that motivate the company.

Hohnen and Potts provided several examples of working definitions of CSR, which included the following illustrative clauses[2]:

> "CSR is the way the company integrates economic, environmental and social objectives while, at the same time, addressing stakeholder expectations and sustaining or enhancing shareholder value."

---

[2] Id. at 24.

"CSR is the overall relationship between the company and its stake-holders, which include customers, employees, communities, owners/investors, government, the general public, communities where the company operates, suppliers and competitors."

"Elements of CSR include investment in community outreach, employee relations, creation and maintenance of employment, environmental stewardship and financial performance."

"CSR means that the company's products and services create value for customers and contribute to the wellbeing of society; the company operates using ethical business practices and expects the same from its suppliers and partners; the company minimizes the environmental impact of its facilities and products; the company provides jobs, pays taxes and makes a profit while supporting philanthropy and community involvement; and the company treats employees with respect and acts as a good neighbor to the people next door as well as those half a world away."

Some companies incorporate one or more the internationally recognized standards and instruments of social responsibility into their working definition of CSR to enhance the legitimacy of the initiative and incorporate widely understood and consistently applied standards of conduct. For example, the working definition of CSR may reference a commitment to adhere to the Ten Principles of the UN Global Compact and may even include brief descriptions of each of the principles that with an explanation of the ways that the company intends to integrate them into its business operations. Whatever method is used to create the working definition, the process is extremely important since it sets a course for all of the activities that will follow during the implementation process and provide a reference point to ensure that all of the policies and practices that are put in place are aligned with the company's goals and objectives.

Identifying Legal Requirements

Another thing to consider as the assessment activities are being planning is the legal and regulatory environment in which the company operates. While CSR is more than an organized effort to comply with minimum legal and regulatory standards applicable to a company's business, the company must nonetheless be sure that it identifies all of the laws and regulations applicable to it and that it already has in place policies and practices designed to ensure compliance. While laws and regulations usually extend beyond the traditional subject matter of CSR efforts, particular emphasis should be placed on assessing compliance in areas such as governance, taxation, bribery and other corrupt practices, conflicts of interest, labor and employment laws, health and safety laws, and environmental laws. Public disclosures of actual or alleged violations of laws and regulations can quickly undermine even the best intended CSR initiative, destroy hard-earned goodwill, and cause long-term reputational damage.

When CSR assessments were first proposed and conducted, there was relatively little to consider with respect to specific legal and regulatory requirements, although certain areas of concern with respect to CSR such as the emissions that might have an adverse environmental impact and safety conditions in the workplace were already subject to scrutiny and legislative and executive actions by lawmakers. However, as time has gone by, the level of regulation has expanded globally, an important trend for companies that operate in foreign markets, and investor interest in CSR has increased, which has caused securities regulators to take a hard look at expanding disclosure requirements to include more CSR-related topics and subjected public companies to greater scrutiny including the need to address shareholder proposals relating to the CSR topics. According to one international law firm writing in 2018, CSR had gone from a "nice to have" to a compliance requirement and applicable regulations could be broken out into three broad categories: disclosure-only, which require companies to discuss whether and how they address a particular issue; those that require companies to put in place compliance programs to address particular CSR issues; and trade-based regulations.[3] The firm noted that not only had regulatory scope expanded, it could also expected that enforcement activities (i.e., litigation and/or governmental investigations) would increase in the years to come, an important shift for those who had long maintained that CSR regulations could largely be ignored

[3] Ropes & Gray, Corporate Social Responsibility Compliance in 2018, and Beyond—An Overview for In-House Legal Counsel (March 12, 2018).

because regulators lacked the resources and/or interest to actually monitor compliance.

The leadership team for the CSR initiative and assessment should include representatives from the company's legal department (or someone from the company's outside law firm serving on a consulting basis in the event that the company does not have in-house counsel) to assist in identifying and analyzing applicable legal and regulatory requirements. In addition, attention should be paid to the development of a CSR compliance legal function that can provide support in identifying and tracking current, pending, and proposed CSR regulations and disclosure requirements. It is important for the company to have one person who becomes the recognized subject matter expert with regard to CSR legal compliance and who can thus coordinate activities of internal and external attorneys from different disciplines (e.g., environmental and employment laws), assume responsibility for defining the scope of the company's CSR compliance program, liaison with various business units, and participate in any working groups established within the organization relating to CSR initiatives and projects.

Reviewing Corporate Documents, Processes, and Activities

A good deal of time during the assessment process will be devoted to reviewing all of the key corporate documents, processes, and activities of the company to identify actual and potential implications of those items to the company's CSR initiatives and programs. The scope of the review will depend on the specific circumstances and the previous actions taken by the company. In general, the review should consider existing mission statements, policies, codes of conduct, principles, and other operating documents; external documents associated with programs or initiatives that the company subscribes, such as sectorwide standards, principles, or guidelines; existing decision-making processes and associated decision-making bodies created by the company to address particular aspects of operations such as worker health and safety and environmental protection; activities of the company that relate directly to providing its products or services to users; activities in other jurisdictions, since operating in foreign countries often carries different challenges in terms of security and conflicts; and activities of business partners, particularly members of the company's supply chain.[4] This is also a good point in the assessment process to collect and review available documents and information on processes and activities for competitors and firms that have been recognized for their CSR efforts in order to benchmark the company's current CSR profile.

The review process should be overseen by members of the leadership team with appropriate experience and expertise in specific CSR-related topics. It is important for reviewers to be aware of best practices in the area including the standards included in international instruments and used by companies that have developed and implemented sophisticated and comprehensive programs and policies in the area. For example, members of the leadership team might use international instruments and the standards of other companies to compile a list of the elements that should be included in a CSR initiative and then compare the company's current practices to this list. This process helps to identify gaps in current practice and also provides the company with a menu of choices that can be used to develop the CSR strategy and identify specific initiatives for each of the company's key stakeholder groups.

In addition to reviewing documents and reports, the team should conduct interviews with key personnel to gain insights into how policies

---

[4] A decision would need to be made about how to classify and categorize existing CSR activities and reference might be made to the methods proposed by Rangan et al., who suggested that CSR programs might be placed into one of three "theaters" for planning purposes: Theater one included philanthropic activities that were primarily motivated by charitable instincts even though they may also have some potential business benefits; Theater two included CSR activities that were symbiotic and intended to simultaneously benefit the company's bottom line and the environmental or social impacts of one or more of company's value chain partners (i.e., the supply chain, distribution channels, or production operations); and Theater three included programs aimed at fundamentally changing the business's ecosystem by taking on short-term risks in order to create social value that ultimately enhance the company's long-term business position. Rangan, K., L. Chase and S. Karim. April 5, 2012. *Why Every Company Needs a CSR Strategy and How to Build It.* Cambridge MA: Harvard Business School Working Paper 12-088.

and practices are really working and should also passively observe activities of company personnel to draw independent conclusions. The review process overlaps with the next step in the assessment process—engaging with key stakeholders—and discussions with stakeholders should include a review of how they are being impacted by the company's current policies and practices.

Identifying and Engaging Key Stakeholders

One of the foundational principles of CSR is engaging and improving relationships with the company's key stakeholders. As such, the assessment must include "stakeholder analysis" through proactive engagement with key internal and external stakeholders to gauge their feelings about CSR generally and the company's specific CSR-related activities, identify their interests, expectations and concerns about their relationship with the company and the company's CSR practices going forward and elicit ideas about improving the company's CSR practices. For example, the concerns of internal stakeholders, such as employees, regarding the company's social and environmental responsibilities need to be identified and analyzed. At the same time, it is essential to determine who the company's most important external stakeholders are and collect information on how those stakeholders have interacted with the company in the past regarding CSR and what their expectations might be with respect to the company's CSR programs. Community concerns are particularly noteworthy even though the company's relationships with other stakeholders, such as investors, customers, lenders, and supply chain partners, have a more direct impact on economic performance. Companies need to reach out to members of their communities through publications, open houses, and workshops to develop and implement ideas about how the company can be a better community member. Finally, the interests and concerns of society in general and regulators should be monitored on a continuous basis and companies should establish and maintain contacts with NGOs, advocates for civil society, legislators, and representatives of regulatory agencies with influence over topics that are relevant to the company.

Hohnen and Potts described stakeholder engagement as the formal and informal ways of staying connected to the parties who have an actual or potential interest in or effect on a company's business (i.e., the company's "stakeholders") and noted that "engagement" implies understanding their views and taking them into consideration, being accountable to them when accountability is called for, and using the information gleaned from them to drive innovation.[5] Stakeholder engagement is related to the fundamental principle of CSR that calls for companies to acknowledge that their businesses do not and cannot exist in isolation and rely heavily on their relationships with customers, employees, suppliers, communities, investors, and others. Stakeholder engagement is more than just listening, although that is obviously very important, but extends to forging working alliances with stakeholders to pursue and achieve mutually agreed results.

Stakeholder engagement is about building relationships with the parties that are most important to sustainability of a company's business. Companies that fail to pay attention to the concerns and opinions of their stakeholders can suddenly find themselves confronted with an array of problems that go to the very heart of their businesses. When companies are unresponsive to their customers, they begin to lose business and revenues tumble. Companies that do not pay attention to the needs of their employees are unable to recruit and retain the talent necessary to remain competitive. Failing to explain strategies and financial performance to investors jeopardizes the availability of capital. Companies that do not stay in touch with the communities in which they are operating will encounter opposition to expansion and other changes that have a local impact. Other important reasons for focusing on engagement include building social capital, reducing risk, driving innovation, integrating

[5] Hohnen, P., and J. Potts, ed. 2007. *Corporate Social Responsibility: An Implementation Guide for Business*, 76–84. (Winnipeg, Canada: International Institute for Sustainable Development, 2007), See also *Stakeholder Engagement: A Good Practice Manual for Doing Business in Emerging Markets* (Washington DC: International Finance Corporation, 2007) and *From Words to Action: The Stakeholder Engagement Manual* (Cobourg, Ontario, Canada: Stakeholder Research Associates in collaboration with AccountaAbility, and the United Nations Environment Programme, 2005).

management, and improved productivity and improving strategic opportunities and access to capital.[6]

The byproduct of the initial engagement process with the various stakeholders should be a detailed description of the needs and expectations, both short and long term, of each of the groups with respect to sustainability-related outcomes of the activities of the company. The description should provide a foundation for analyzing how the activities of the company impact each of the stakeholder groups, either positively or negatively, and allow the company to create a scorecard for its stakeholder relationships that can provide ideas for specific initiatives and serve as a tracking system for performance. Including long-term needs of stakeholder groups is consistent with the principle of sustainable development that underpins CSR and requires sophisticated scenario analysis that takes into account a wide range of potential future paths and events.

Identifying and Measuring Economic, Social, and Environmental Impacts

One of the key questions that should be asked and answered as the company collects and analyzes information in order to assess its current status with respect to CSR activities is whether the company is doing a good job of identifying its main economic, social, and environmental impacts. For example, does the company have processes in place to measure profitability and the economic value that its activities generate for its shareholders, employees, and the communities in which it operates and society in general (e.g., through taxes paid on profits that are used for public services). With regard to social impacts, the company should be able to identify and measure the impact that its operational and philanthropic activities, including volunteer work by company employees, is have on local communities and the positive impacts that its products and services are having on the social well-being of its customers. Finally, environmental impact can be understood and measured by tracking indicators such as carbon

---

[6] Hohnen, P. (Author) and J. Potts (Editor), *Corporate Social Responsibility: An Implementation Guide for Business* (Winnipeg, Canada: International Institute for Sustainable Development, 2007), 76–84.

emissions, water usage, and waste production. When measuring impacts, consideration should also be given to the activities of members of the company's supply chain (e.g., contracts with suppliers may create a significant number of new jobs up and down the supply chain and enhance the revenues and overall profitability of the suppliers). A similar indirect economic impact can be seen and appreciated when measures are taken of the jobs created in local communities due to the presence of the company's operational facilities (e.g., restaurants and other service providers established to meet the needs of the company's employees).

When assessing current economic, social, and environmental impacts, reference should be made to the financial records of the company, focusing on both strengths and weaknesses; the company contractual obligations and the current state of affairs with respect to contract compliance by both the company and its contract partners; and quantitative and qualitative measures of energy usage, water usage, waste disposal, and emissions related to the company activities. Larger companies with multiple business units and/or foreign subsidiaries should establish global standards and impact metrics that can be used by each of the business units and subsidiaries to conduct their own assessments appropriate adjusts for local practices and programs and sector-specific issues. The global standards and impact metrics that apply across all of the units can be used for internal benchmarking purposes and identifying which parts of the larger organization are doing a better or worse job with respect to a particular issue. Tasking each unit with measuring impacts in all of the areas also ensures that they consider all of the CSR issues that have been identified as important by senior leadership and not just those that are of interest to the managers of those units.

The information collected in order to compare the company's current situation with respect to economic, social, and environmental impacts can be used in later stages of the CSR launch process, such as when the company needs to set its CSR strategy, make its CSR commitments, and set associated performance targets and develop a CSR reporting and communications system. The results of the inventory and assessment should be formally compiled into a written report that identifies the scale of the company's economic, social, and environmental impact. Before finalizing the report, input should be sought from key stakeholders to ensure that their expectations regarding impact measurement have been taken into account. Impact assessment should not be limited to internal activities, but should also include positive and negative impacts associated with the activities of supply chain partners as they contribute to the company's value chain.

Identifying and Prioritizing Key CSR Activities

The assessment process should be all-inclusive in order to provide organizational leaders with the information needed in order to make important decisions regarding the direction of the organization's CSR activities. Once the information from the assessment process has been largely collected, the team should turn its attention to identifying and prioritizing the activities associated with the organization's environmental and social responsibility. The first step at this stage is an extensive due diligence process in order to understand where and how the organization's activities impact the environment and society, a topic that has been discussed earlier. The next step is to identify and define the CSR themes and issues that are most relevant and significant to the organization's success. Finally, the themes and issues identified in the previous step need to be prioritized in light of limitations on resources that all organizations, regardless of size, must contend with when deciding on the most effective way to implement CSR.

Understanding the Organization's Social Responsibilities

Section 7.3.1 of ISO 26000 describes a due diligence process that organizations should follow in order to gain a better understanding of their social responsibilities. Due diligence was explained to be a comprehensive, proactive process to identify the actual and potential negative social, environmental, and economic impacts of an organization's decisions and activities, with the aim of avoiding and mitigating those impacts as well as efforts to influence the behavior of others where they are found to be the cause of human rights or other violations in which the organization may be implicated. The due diligence process outlined in Section 7.3.1

included the following components, which should be addressed in a manner that is appropriate to the organization's size and circumstances[7]:

- Organizational policies related to the relevant core subject that give meaningful guidance to those within the organization and those closely linked to the organization
- Means of assessing how existing and proposed activities may affect those policy goals
- Means of integrating social responsibility core subjects throughout the organization
- Means of tracking performance over time, to be able to make necessary adjustments in priorities and approach
- Appropriate actions to address the negative impacts of its decisions and activities

Determining the Relevance and Significance of Core CSR Subjects and Issues

The core subjects of CSR and their related issues span the entire spectrum of human and business activities and all of the subjects have some degree of relevance for every organization; however, as pointed out in Section 7.3.2.1 of ISO 26000, not all of the issues are relevant to a particular organization and the need to effectively invest scarce time and resources means that each organization must carefully identify and prioritize those issues that are most significant to its specific sustainability and CSR efforts.[8] The process recommended by ISO 26000 begins with the identification of potential issues by doing the following[9]:

- Cataloging the full range of the organization's activities
- Identifying the organization's stakeholders

---

[7] ISO 26000 Guidance on Social Responsibility (Geneva: International Organization for Standardization, 2010), 71.

[8] Id. at 72.

[9] Id.

- Identifying the activities of the organization itself and of the organization within its sphere of influence (e.g., suppliers and contractors)
- Determining which core subjects and issues might arise when the organization and others within the sphere of influence and/or the value chain carry out these activities, taking into account all applicable legislation
- Examining the range of ways in which the organization's decisions and activities can cause impacts on stakeholders and on sustainable development
- Examining the ways in which stakeholders and social responsibility issues can impact the decisions, activities and plans of the organization
- Identifying all issues of social responsibility that relate to day-to-day activities as well as those that arise only occasionally under very specific circumstances

Most of the information for identification of issues should have been collected and catalogued during the afore-described assessment phase. Views should be solicited from throughout the organization, and ISO 26000 recommended that organizations supplement their self-evaluation during the identification process with inputs from key stakeholders in order to broaden the perspective on the core subjects and issues and cautioned organizations not to assume that compliance with applicable laws will be sufficient to adequately address a particular problem or issue, particularly in cases where laws and regulations are not well enforced or sufficiently detailed. In fact, many issues associated with social responsibility, such as providing work–life balance to workers and investing in workers' professional development, are rarely covered by laws and regulations.[10]

No doubt the list of potential social responsibility issues will be lengthy and comprehensive and the next job for the organization is to begin the prioritization process by deciding which of the issues have the greatest

---

[10] Id.

significance and are most important to the organization. Section 7.3.2 of ISO 26000 suggests that organizations sort and edit their lists by applying criteria such as the extent of the impact of the issue on stakeholders and sustainable development; the potential effect of taking action or failing to take action on the issue; the level of stakeholder concern about the issue; the identification of the societal expectations of responsible behavior concerning these impacts; and, in the case of issues related to the organization's relationships with value chain partners, the organization's realistic ability to exert its influence on the partner. ISO 26000 noted that, in general, the most material issues will be those that involve noncompliance with laws and regulations; inconsistency with recognized international standards and norms of behavior; potential violations of human rights; practices that could endanger life or health; and practices that could have a serious negative effect on the environment.[11]

Prioritization

Once the initial list has been managed and reduced by looking at issues through the lens of significance, the next step is to establish priorities among the remaining issues so that strategies, commitments, targets and measurement, and reporting processes can be established and/or adjusted. The order of priorities will vary among organizations and input from stakeholders should be solicited at this stage. Section 7.3.4 of ISO 26000 recommended that the following criteria be applied during the prioritization process: the current performance of the organization with regard to legal compliance, international standards, international norms of behavior, the state-of-the-art and best practice; whether the issue can significantly affect the ability of the organization to meet important objectives; the potential effect of the related action compared to the resources required for implementation; the length of time to achieve the desired results; whether there can be significant cost implications if not addressed quickly; and the ease and speed of implementation, which may have a bearing on increasing awareness of and motivation for action on social responsibility within the organization.

---

[11] Id.

The primary goal of prioritization is to establish an agenda for current action; however, priorities will obviously change as time goes by and organizations must regularly revisit and update their list of priority issues. When prioritizing issues, special notice should be taken of projects that may not make the current list but which the organization wants to reconsider at some point in the future, such as constructing new facilities, expanding the workforce, or raising capital to fund additional CSR-related activities.[12] Priorities can also change quickly, often without much warning, as a result of external events relating to the organization directly and/or a key stakeholder of the organization. For example, an issue regarding the safety of one of the organization's products should always be given a high priority, particularly since the adverse reputational impact associated with the issue can be significant and immediate. Another situation in which organizational priorities should be reassessed is when a natural disaster occurs in the community in which the organization is operating. In those cases, the organization will be expected to proactively divert resources to assist the community and its members (including the organization's own employees and their families).

---

[12] *ISO 26000 Guidance on Social Responsibility* (Geneva: International Organization for Standardization, 2010), 74.

CHAPTER 4

Developing a Corporate Social Responsibility Strategy

The collection and analysis of information during the assessment stage is valuable in and of itself in that it necessarily increases awareness of the potential role of social responsibility in the company's business activities allows the company to benchmark its corporate social responsibility (CSR) profile against the efforts of competitors and learn more about the needs and expectations of its stakeholders and identify and prioritize its own unique set of CSR issues and actions. However, the primary purpose of the assessment is to provide the leadership team with the information necessary for it to develop a CSR strategy. As with any other strategic initiative, CSR activities must be institutionalized into the organization in order to be sustainable and thus it is essential that CSR be seen to be inherent in the organizational culture and adopted as part of the company's long-term strategy and decision making rather than being seen as an "add on" that can be discarded when circumstances change (e.g., when an economic downturn creates pressures to divert resources away from sustainability initiatives).[1] Like any other strategy, a CSR strategy reflects decisions among multiple potential CSR projects and provides a path for implementation, assigns roles and responsibilities throughout the organization, establishes timetables for the completion of various tasks and incorporates metrics to measure progress and performance. The CSR strategy should reflect the consideration of the company's strengths and weaknesses and the opportunities and threats identified during the

---

[1] Maon, F., V. Swaen and A. Lindgreen. 2008. *Mainstreaming the Corporate Responsibility Agenda: A Change Model Grounded in Theory and Practice*, 37. IAG- Louvain School of Management Working Paper.

assessment phase and must also be aligned with the company's core values and standards.

While there are certain elements that should be included in a formal version of a company's CSR strategy, the process itself should remain fluid and flexible in order to elicit participation from all of the company's stakeholders in a dialogue that begins by focusing on just what CSR means to the company. Strategy development must be proactively led by the senior leaders of the company since they are responsible for setting the appropriate tone, allocating the resources necessary to implement the strategy once it is in place and ensuring that the strategic targets are understood by everyone in the organization and embedded into the company's culture and systems. When developing the strategy, attention should be paid to creating a record of meetings and other discussions that were integral to development process since the record itself can be a valuable resources for preserving ideas and providing evidence to stakeholders that serious consideration has been given to CSR strategy and decision making.

The strategy itself should include a mission statement, goals and commitments, and policies for each of the CSR dimensions covered by the strategy (e.g., financial, environmental, labor, community, and supply chain responsibility), key performance indicators, a clear allocation of responsibilities for the implementation of the strategy and procedures for reporting on progress, and regular evaluation of the strategy. As the strategy moves toward finalization, it should circulated to key stakeholders for their input, a step that not only improves the strategy but creates a sense of participation among stakeholders that will ultimately garner their support. Once the company is actively engaged in implementing the strategy, it is essential to measure and assure performance, engage stakeholders and report on performance, both internally and externally. The CSR leadership team must evaluate performance, identify opportunities for improvement, and engage with stakeholders on implementing changes.

According to Hohnen and Potts, a good CSR strategy typically identifies the overall direction for where the firm wants to take its CSR work; the stakeholders and their perspectives and interests; a basic approach for moving ahead; specific priority areas; a timeline for action, responsible staff, and immediate next steps; and a process for reviewing and assuring outcomes.[2] As for the process of developing a CSR strategy, Hohnen and Potts suggested the following steps[3]:

- Build support with the CEO, senior management, and employees
- Conduct an analysis of risks and strengths, weaknesses, threats, and opportunities
- Research what others (including competitors) are doing
- Assess the value of recognized voluntary CSR instruments
- Developing and prioritizing options for proposed CSR activities
- Building a business case for each of the proposed CSR activities
- Decide on direction, approach, boundaries, and focus areas

Building Support With Senior Management and Employees

CSR initiatives will not be successful without the strong and continuing support of senior management and employees. Hopefully the collection of information during the assessment process, including dialogue among the members of the leadership team and between those team members and employees and other stakeholders, has built an awareness of the potential opportunities associated with socially and environmentally responsible business activities. This awareness should serve as the foundation for support of the development and implementation of the actual CSR strategy. In particular, support needs to be gathered for sometimes difficult changes in product and service offerings and changes to decision-making processes and organizational structure. Change management is the responsibility of senior management and senior managers must be willing to add CSR activities to their already busy schedules. One way to create "buy in" among senior managers is to get them involved in stakeholder engagement at a very early stage since those conversations generally uncover opportunities that senior management will be eager to integrate into their strategies.

---

[2] Hohnen, P., and J. Potts, ed. 2007. *Corporate Social Responsibility: An Implementation Guide for Business,* 32–33. Winnipeg, Canada: International Institute for Sustainable Development.

[3] Id. at 33.

People at all levels of the organizational hierarchy may be asked to take on new roles and responsibilities and, as noted earlier, the leadership team must be prepared to "make the case for change" and provide incentives to employees for wholehearted participation in the CSR initiative. Some of those incentives will be actual changes and improvements to the day-to-day experience of employees such as more training and mentoring opportunities and implementation of work–life balance policies. Other steps that should be taken to build employee support include involving employees in business decisions that affect them and improve the work environment. Particular attention should be paid to engaging middle management personnel, many of whom may be skeptical of the importance and relevance of CSR, and steps that should be taken include sharing the business case for proposed CSR actions with impacted middle managers to demonstrate how the actions will have a positive influence on the resources they oversee. The business case should also describe the support that middle managers can expect to receive to help them carry out their new CSR-related responsibilities.

Situation ("SWOT") Analysis

Once the company has collected and screened all the relevant information about its external environment and its own internal resources, a thorough analysis should be undertaken to match the strengths of the company to opportunities in the business environment and identify weaknesses that are likely to create challenges to the company's efforts to execute its strategies and attain its goals and objectives. One well-known and useful tool for this process is referred to as "SWOT analysis," sometimes referred to as "situation analysis," so named because it calls for systematic review of the company's strengths and weaknesses and the opportunities and threats in the company's business environment as a means for uncovering strategies that effectively leverage the company's core competencies. In general, SWOT analysis involves the following five steps:

- The analyst should begin by scanning the company's external environment in order to develop an overall point of reference for the analysis of opportunities and threats that will follow.

There are a number of potential sources of information such as business partners, including internal and external customers, suppliers, and distributors; governmental entities (local, state, federal, and international); professional or trade associations (conventions and exhibitions); and journals and reports, including scientific and professional journals that include information on relevant technologies.

- The second step is identifying and evaluating the company's strengths with an eye toward determining just what attributes and resources might provide the company with a sustainable competitive advantage. Strengths might include "world-class" manufacturing capabilities, a strong intellectual property portfolio, skilled and talented employees, significant market share in a key market, access to capital, and/or strong goodwill and reputation among customers and other business partners.

- The third step is identifying and evaluating the company's weaknesses with an eye toward identifying issues that might materially impair the ability of the company to achieve its strategic goals and objectives and compete effectively in its chosen markets. Weaknesses are generally defined in relation to recognizable strengths of competitors and may crop in the form of inadequate facilities and/or an outdated and weak intellectual property portfolio.

- While the second and third steps—identification of strengths and weaknesses—are based primarily on an internal assessment, the fourth step of identifying opportunities calls for a full and creative exploration of the company's external environment. Opportunities generally include emerging markets and technologies as well as existing markets where competitors are failing to satisfy the needs of customers or which are expected to grow sufficiently to comfortably allow new entrants.

- The final step is identifying characteristics of the company's external environment that are likely to threaten the company's competitive position in the future. Of particular interest would be events that would threaten the company's existing customer relationships such as new competitors, changing customer requirements, and development and introduction of substitute products.

Threats may also emerge from new regulations, input shortages, or development of new technologies.

While all the steps in the SWOT analysis is important, the most crucial questions generally relate to whether or not the company is able to identify resources and other factors that can offer it a sustainable and reasonably protectable competitive advantage. An identifiable tangible or intangible asset, such as a patent or exclusive licensing arrangement, is certainly a good source of competitive advantage; however, it is important to think broadly at this stage to consider other possibilities that may be difficult to quantify. For example, a small emerging company often has an advantage over larger firms because of its ability to respond more quickly to opportunities in the marketplace. This "flexibility" advantage can and should be leveraged in a way that allows the company to quickly and efficiently introduce new products and services. Many emerging companies also derive a competitive advantage from the people that they attract to work for them and senior management should not ignore the role that the human resources function can play in creating and executing an effective strategy.

Weaknesses identified during the SWOT analysis should also be taken seriously and companies must be prepared to identify and implement significant changes to their strategy rather than continuing down a road that will ultimately be unsuccessful in light of the entrenched position of competitors or significant hurdles in the company's external environment. Assume, for example, that the SWOT analysis indicates that a large competitor has been able to build a significant cost advantage based on proprietary technology that the competitor introduced after several years of development. Assuming that the company's intellectual property position with the technology is strong it would make no sense for the company to attempt to compete on the basis of price or undertake a lengthy and expensive research and development program to create its own technology that would threaten the competitor's position. In that situation the weakness in relation to the competitor dictates that the company should look elsewhere for its strategic initiatives. One possibility would be concentrating on new product lines where the competitor's technological lead is not relevant and in which the company's own competitive advantages can be fully exploited.

The value of SWOT analysis to the strategic planning process is that it forces senior management to fully understand the company's external environment and critically evaluate the company's own internal strengths and weaknesses. While companies often choose to leverage their strengths in areas where of the external environment where competition is sparse, there may also be situations where the information in the SWOT analysis clarifies that the company's strengths are adequate to allow for head-to-head competition with other businesses for a piece of what is clearly the most profitable market available to the company at that time. SWOT analysis should also disclose opportunities for the company to make changes in its external environment that will make it easier to exploit its strengths. For example, the company may decide it is in its interest to proactively lobby for changes in applicable laws and regulations in a way that will open new market opportunities that fit well with the company competitive advantages. Before any strategy is set, however, the information from the analysis should be used to sketch out several alternative scenarios that can be evaluated and compared side-by-side.

Obviously SWOT analysis can contribute to the developing the most appropriate overall strategy for the company—one that aligns the company's strengths (i.e., competitive advantages) to the most promising opportunities in the company's external environment. The information collected during the SWOT analysis can also be quite valuable to the company for other reasons. For example, as the company learns more about its competitors, it can begin to establish benchmarks to compare its performance and resources in key areas against that of other firms. This provides opportunities for companies to learn and absorb best practices from other firms with regard to functional activities that can become the basis for a competitive advantage. In situations where the gap between the company and its competitors is extreme an important part of the company's overall strategic goals and objectives may well be acquiring and deploying the resources necessary to close that gap. Benchmarking itself is a complicated mix of art and science and performance measures should be identified with respect to the efficiency of particular processes and the results obtained by the firm from using those processes.

Researching CSR Activities of Other Firms and Existing CSR Instruments

Information from research on CSR activities of other firms and existing CSR instruments should have been collected duringthe afore-discussed assessmentphase as a means for measuring how the company's current CSR efforts compare to similar companies and recognized international standards and best practices. When attention turns to developing the CSR strategy, these same sources of information should be viewed as valuable precedents from others with substantial experience in the area and should be mined to identify the areas of greatest import and gather ideas that can be incorporated into the company's own CSR strategy.[4]

The leadership team should closely assess the CSR activities of two types of companies: companies that operate in the same countries and markets (i.e., competitors) and companies that have gained a reputation for sound CSR practices even though they cannot reasonably be considered competitors of the company. In each case, the goal is to figure out what those companies are doing with respect to CSR and identify similarities and differences between those firms and the company. Information should be available from public statements regarding vision, values, and policies; codes of conduct; marketing materials for products and services and social responsibility reports prepared and published as part of the firm's governance program. While other firms will not disclose all the details of their various projects, the leadership team should be able to get a good sense of the benefits, costs, and projected outcomes of a particular initiatives, assess how they might be implemented by the company, and identify key changes in organizational practices that will be needed in order for a comparable project to be launched.

Research on what other companies are doing should be carried out by members of the leadership team that already have operational experience in developing and implementing comparable CSR initiatives as they are the people best situation to "fill in the gaps" given that it is generally not feasible to get all the information necessary to fully understand what

---

[4] One useful tool for researching CSR activities of other firms is Pivot Goals, which is a database of the sustainability goals of the world's largest and leading companies (http://pivotgoals.com/about.php).

other companies are doing. Looking at what competitors might be doing makes sense from a broader strategic perspective since it is always important to be scanning the moves of other firms and it is generally easier to make comparisons with competitors since many aspects of their operational activities are similar and already known to the company. As for information from noncompetitive companies, the goal is to expand the leadership team's knowledge of "best practices" and then figure out what specific lessons can be drawn and put to work in the company's particular situation. Several organizations regularly publish lists of companies considered to be leaders in corporate responsibility and sustainability. In addition, information on best practices relating to CSR can be collected from industry associations and CSR specialist organizations such as the World Business Council for Sustainable Development (www.wbscd.org), Business for Social Responsibility (www.bsr.org), and the Conference Board (www.conference-board.org), all of which conduct research, hold conferences, and workshops and issue newsletters and other publications on CSR issues.[5]

Assessing the Relevance and Value of Voluntary CSR Instruments

Compliance with laws is a fundamental principle of environmental and social responsibility; however, much of CSR is based on aspiring to fulfill principles and standards that extend beyond what has been formally approved in a legislative or regulatory process. ISO 26000, promulgated by the International Organization for Standards, noted that an important and effective way to accelerate the implementation of CSR is by tapping into the resources and credibility of one or more of the many organizations that have developed voluntary initiatives and instruments, and even launched separate organizations, intended to help other organizations seeking to become more socially responsible. The goal of these initiatives has generally been to develop a consensus among disparate groups (i.e.,

[5] Hohnen, P., and J. Potts, ed. 2007. *Corporate Social Responsibility: An Implementation Guide for Business*, 35. Winnipeg, Canada: International Institute for Sustainable Development.

governmental organizations, the business community, nongovernmental organizations, and other experts) regarding international norms and standards with respect to various areas that are commonly placed beneath the expansive umbrella of CSR.

According to ISO 26000, some of these initiatives address aspects of one or more core subjects or issues, while others cover various ways that social responsibility can be integrated into an organization's decisions and activities and create or promote specific tools or practical guides that can be used for integrating social responsibility throughout an organization. Another common activity of these initiatives is the development or promotion of minimum standards and expectations regarding some aspect of social responsibility such as codes of conduct, recommendations, guidelines, declarations of principles, and value statements. These standards may be "universal" (i.e., applicable to all organizations) or sector-specific and thus tailored to unique conditions and issues in a particular sector. Some initiatives also involve the possibility of certification against the standards in the initiative by independent third parties.[6]

Annex A to ISO 26000 contains a nonexhaustive list of voluntary initiatives and tools for social responsibility that were identified by the ISO 26000 working group experts during the development of ISO 26000 using a specific set of criteria that is also described in Annex A.[7] Annex A distinguished between cross-sectoral and sectoral initiatives (i.e., initiatives that have been developed by specific sectors such as agriculture, information technology, public services, tourism etc,). Three types of cross-sectoral initiatives were identified: "intergovernmental initiatives" (i.e., developed and administered by intergovernmental organizations, such as the UN Global Compact); "multistakeholder initiatives" (i.e., developed or administered through multistakeholder processes, such as the AccountAbility AA 1000 Series, the Ceres Principles, and Transparency International); and "single-stakeholder initiatives" (i.e., developed or administered through single-stakeholder processes, such as the Caux

[6] 2010. *ISO 26000 Guidance on Social Responsibility*, 83. Geneva: International Organization for Standardization.
[7] Id. at 86.

Round Table Principles for Business, and the World Business Council for Sustainable Development).

Many organizations find that attaching themselves to one or more of the well-known voluntary CSR initiatives is a good way to organize and announce their CSR commitments. For example, companies of all sizes have pledged their support for the Organisation for Economic Co-operation and Development (OECD) Guidelines for Multinational Enterprises, the International Labour Organization's Declaration on Fundamental Principles and Rights at Work, the United Nations Global Compact, ISO 26000, and other standards established by the ISO and the Global Reporting Initiative. Sector- and industry-specific codes and guidelines may also be available for companies depending on their line of business (e.g., tools, codes, and standards on sustainable development and CSR for the mineral exploration industry developed by the Prospectors and Developers Association of Canada). However, Section 7.8.2 of ISO 26000 made the point that it was not necessary for an organization to participate in any of the initiatives for social responsibility, or to use any of their tools, in order for it to be socially responsible, nor was participation necessarily a reliable indicator of the social responsibility of an organization.

Initiatives vary significantly with respect to their credibility in the eyes of stakeholders and many are generally perceived as being little more than a public relations scheme designed to protect the reputation of members as opposed to helping them make real progress toward social responsibility. Participation in any of these initiatives comes with a cost in terms of time, effort, and resources and organizations need to determine whether participation will be perceived as valuable by their stakeholders and provide them with access to practical guidance that can be readily used to drive implementation and integration of CSR. Section 7.8.3 of ISO 26000 includes the following list of factors that organizations should take into account when considering whether to participate in or use a CSR initiative[8]:

---

[8] Id. at 84.

- Whether the initiative is consistent with ISO 26000's principles of social responsibility (i.e., accountability, transparency, ethical behavior and respect for stakeholder interests, the rule of law, international norms of behavior, and human rights)
- Whether the initiative provides valuable and practical guidance to assist the organization to address a particular core subject or issue and/or to integrate social responsibility throughout its activities
- Whether the initiative is designed for that particular type of organization or its areas of interest
- Whether the initiative is locally or regionally applicable, or whether it has global scope and whether it applies to all types of organizations
- Whether the initiative will assist the organization to reach specific stakeholder groups
- The kind of organization or organizations that developed and govern the initiative, such as government, NGO, labor, private sector, or academic
- The reputation of the organization or organizations that developed and govern the initiative, considering their credibility and integrity
- The nature of the process for developing and governing the initiative (e.g., whether the initiative has been developed through or governed by a multistakeholder, transparent, open, and accessible process, with developed and developing country participants)
- The accessibility of the initiative (e.g., whether an organization must sign a contract to participate, or whether there are costs to join the initiative)

Developing and Prioritizing Options for Proposed CSR Actions and Activities

The assessment of the company's current and potential CSR activities, combined with the survey of practices of other companies and guidelines included in CSR instruments, should allow the leadership team to start putting together a list of proposed CSR actions that can then be analyzed in light of the company's immediate opportunities and threats and available resources. One approach to identifying and prioritizing pro-posed CSR actions is to begin by collecting and placing ideas into an L-shaped matrix: one dimension would be the main categories of CSR activities (i.e., environmental, social (e.g., workers, communities), and economic (e.g., quality assurance, customer satisfaction)) and the other dimension would be the element of the company's activities that would be the focal point of the action (i.e., processes, such as upgrading regis-tration and certification status; products and services such as focusing on product labeling and performance characteristics; and impacts such as increasing stakeholder engagement). Another important step is to hold brainstorming sessions with key internal and external stakeholders including members of the senior management team, employees, and rep-resentatives from key business partners and the surrounding community to understand their expectations, intensity of interest, and willingness and ability to contribute to strategy execution.

A different perspective can be gleaned from mapping the CSR land-scape based on two dimensions—benefit to society and benefit to busi-ness—and then populating that map with suggested activities based on where they fall among four areas: "pet projects," activities selected by indi-vidual executives based on their personal interests, are often supported by companies, yet typically have little benefit to either society or the busi-ness; philanthropy, which generally does well in terms of benefit to society but often provides little in the way of business benefit unless done stra-tegically; "propaganda" activities that are primarily intended to enhance the company's reputation but do not produce much in the way of social benefit and often put the company at risk for criticism if it appears that its actions are not as strong as it words; and "partnering" arrangements established to improve the company's core value creation abilities, address long-term challenges to the company's sustainability, and make an impact on important social issues such as improving employment, overall quality of life, and living standards. Mapping of this type highlights shortcoming in prior actions and illustrates how companies can shift the balance of their activities toward strategic philanthropy and high value and impact-ful partnering initiatives.

Another approach the leadership team should use to develop options for new CSR actions is to hold brainstorming sessions with key internal and external stakeholders including members of the senior management team, employees, and representatives from key business partners and the surrounding community. The foundation for these sessions should have been established during the dialogue that began in the assessment stage. While the agenda for the sessions might vary a good starting point would be to go through the following questions recommended by Hohnen and Potts[9]:

- What social and environmental activities and initiatives has the company undertaken already?
- What strengths, weaknesses, opportunities, and threats do these present?
- What has the company learned from others that could be helpful?
- What are the company's CSR goals?
- Where could the company be in terms of CSR activities and outcomes five and ten years down the road?
- What are the big social issues and how might the company help?
- If the company is to be a CSR leader, what changes to current practices and products would need to take place?
- Are there some CSR activities or initiatives the company could easily undertake now at no or low cost (i.e., is there any "low hanging fruit")?
- Are there areas in which CSR changes would have a particularly big impact on the company and others? What are they and what are the likely impacts?
- Can the proposed CSR changes be organized into short-, medium- and long-term deliverables?
- What are the resource implications of these deliverables?
- Are there any changes to the company's organizational structure that would need to occur to implement any of the deliverables?
- Are there any other obstacles or impediments (e.g., inadequate training or equipment or inappropriate incentive structures) that might stand in the way of taking a more systematic approach to implementing CSR? If so, what are they?

---

[9] Id. at 38.

- Are there opportunities for cost reductions?
- What are the potential risks of failing to take into account the broader environmental, social, and economic aspects of the company's activities?
- What should be the priorities for action if the company decides to do more?

As previously noted, the brainstorming sessions can and should contribute to strengthening stakeholder relationships, engagement, and collaboration. In addition, the opportunity to participate in discussing what are often difficult issues builds commitment and excitement among those involved and makes it easier for participants to "take ownership" of the ideas and champion them throughout the organization once the time comes for implementation. Some companies use outside facilitators for these sessions in order to take advantage of their expertise in group dynamics and eliciting comments and provide a neutrality that ensures that the "agenda" of any one person or business unit does not skew the process and ignore other good ideas. Outside sources may be used to gather information necessary to answer some of the questions posed earlier. For example, while participants may have their own views about what are the most pressing social and environmental issues reference should also be made to publicly available surveys on the subject in order to get a better idea of stakeholder expectations and the likelihood of changes in regulatory and market attitudes.

Regardless of the approach that is taken by a company, the leadership team needs to remain focused on materiality in order to manage what will typically be a long list of potential ideas that, taken together, would overwhelm the company's available resources if all of them were executed simultaneously. While many companies appears to have a wide range of programs that they proudly promote as indicators of their environmental and social responsibility—biking programs, recycling drives, and small philanthropic initiatives selected based on the preferences of the CEO— they fail to achieve the level of success they might have if they limited their efforts to a handful of impactful projects around material business and sustainability issues that can be clearly measured and explained to stakeholders. This does not mean that companies, particularly small businesses, should not bother with modest programs to get their feet wet; however, the long-term goal should be to undertake and realize dramatic and fundamental changes in business models, products, processes, and stakeholder relationships to incorporate socially and environmentally responsible principles.

Building the Business Case for a Proposed CSR Action

While CSR is grounded in the fundamental proposition that companies should look beyond economic performance to take into account the social and environmental impact of their activities, the reality is that "doing the right thing" is not a sufficient argument and CSR initiatives also need to make good business sense and be based on economic, environmental, and social goals that are achievable and that do not create undue risk to the survival of the company. All this means that the leadership team should be creating and evaluate a business case for each of the CSR ideas that a company is considering; however, research indicates that only about one in four companies that have decided to formally pursue a sustainability strategy have taken the extra time to establish the necessary business case. Among the companies that do take the time to develop a business case, many take a reactive approach and wait until it is necessary to respond to external pressures (i.e., "playing defense" and focusing their sustainability activities and investments on mitigating risk and other externalities, preserving reputation and regulatory compliance). The preferred assumption for building a CSR business case is that the investment should be perceived in the same way as any other opportunity, which means demonstrating how the project will increase market share, enhance efficiencies, and create a competitive advantage. Having a strong business case that has been rigorously vetted supports other key requirements for effective CSR including leadership commitment, employee engagement and interest, and clear goals and metrics that can be readily communicated and stakeholder engagement and support.

Deciding on Direction, Approach, and Focus Areas

Once the most promising and interesting CSR actions have been identified and business cases created for each of them, the leadership team
needs to decide on the direction, approach, and focus areas of the CSR
initiative. In many cases, a proposed action will be eliminated after the
business case is completed and it is clear that undertaking the action is not
feasible. The business case analysis will generally allow the leadership team
to create a rough ranking of the proposals from an economic perspective;
however, it is not always the case that these rankings are followed and
an action that may not have as strong a business case as the others may
still be selected because it fills a gap in building on a relationship with an
important stakeholder group. Ultimately the choices must be based on
the size and importance of the issue addressed by the proposed action,
the chances of success for the proposed action, and the degree of diffi-
culty in implementing the action, the amount of time that will likely pass
before results are seen from the action, the financial and human resources
required to effectively implement the action and the anticipated legal,
political, technological, and cultural hurdles to implementing the action.
In addition, consideration needs to be given to feasibility of support from
outside parties. For example, many good ideas for developing countries
are simply not viable unless and until local governments make improvements to roads and telecommunications.

Hohnen and Potts explained that the "direction" is the overall course
that the company could pursue or the main areas it is aiming to address.[10]
While the answer to this question should be consistent with generally
recognized values and standards (e.g., protecting human rights or the
environment), it will also very company-specific. Examples of a "direction" include emphasizing worker health and safety; for pharmaceutical
companies, focusing on health issues in developing countries; environmental issues associated with manufacturing processes; relations with
surrounding communities; and implementing antibribery measures. The
"approach" includes the steps that the company intends to take in order

---

[10] The discussion in this paragraph is adapted from Hohnen, P., and J. Potts, ed.
2007. *Corporate Social Responsibility: An Implementation Guide for Business*, 40.
Winnipeg, Canada: International Institute for Sustainable Development.

to proceed in the selected direction and might include revising its mission, creating and implementing new codes of conducts, employee communications, and training and engagement with supply chain partners. Finally, "focus areas" should be clearly aligned with the company's business objectives and thus an immediate priority. Examples include changes in the company's existing processes (i.e., that is, enhanced protection of personal information by a financial institution), investment in new opportunities (i.e., a bank launching microcredit programs in developing countries), and/or implementation of new programs to address critical needs of key stakeholders (i.e., a food retailer introducing new products to help customers in the battle with obesity).

There are a number of different ways to develop a "strategy" and the key point is that the parties involved need to have the skills and experience necessary, including knowledge about the company' external environment, to develop a top-line sustainability approach, focus areas, and goals and targets (including a means for measuring progress toward achievement of the goals and targets). For example, on the section of its website relating to sustainability strategy (www.gesustainability.com) General Electric (GE) described its top-line sustainability approach as "investing in developing sustainable and environment-friendly products to drive revenue growth." In executing its strategy, GE focused on three areas: developing a safe working environment, developing products that met customers' needs, and supporting society through social activities. Specific goals and targets, which were measured and reporting on regularly, were established for workforce development and inclusiveness, governance, health and safety, health, energy and climate, water, charitable giving, volunteering, and investment in innovation.

Another example is provided by the public positions of Kellogg Company, which declared in 2012 that it was "devoted to producing great-tasting foods that people love, and to operating all aspects of our business safely and responsibly."[11] Kellogg broke its global CSR strategies into four categories, each of which had their own issues:

[11] See Kellogg 2012. "Corporate Responsibility Report, http://kelloggcompany. com/content/dam/kelloggcompanyus/corporate_responsibility/pdf/2012/2012_ Kelloggs_CRR.pdf (accessed April 20, 2018).

- *Marketplace:* Kellogg committed to continuing to be seen as a trusted provider of "great-tasting, safe, and high-quality products" and a company that contributed to the health and nutrition of its consumers by providing food products that they could integrate as part of a balanced diet and that met their varying taste requirements. Kellogg also committed to creating and practicing ethical and responsible marketing standards and ensuring that consumers had access to the information necessary to make informed choices.
- *Environment:* Kellogg committed to the pursuit of sustainable growth through the protection and conservation of natural resources and set goals and targets with respect to reducing the environmental footprint of its products, achieving cost savings throughout the value chain, increasing the recycled content of packaging, and building the company's understanding of sustainable agriculture practices that align with the company's business needs for the procurement of ingredients, ensuring required quality, traceability, nutritional content, and continuity of supply.
- *Workplace:* Kellogg committed to support a talented and dedicated workforce and foster a work environment that valued diversity and inclusion and aimed to reflect the diversity of our consumer demographics. In addition, Kellogg committed to remaining competitive with respect to compensation, being a leader in its sector in health and safety performance and ensuring that suppliers upheld the same labor standards that the company expected of its own operations.
- *Community:* Building on its belief in "the power of breakfast to feed better days and better lives," Kellogg's commitment with respect to global charitable giving efforts were focused on providing servings of cereal and snacks, more than half of which would be breakfasts, to those who needed it most.

Kellogg noted that the specific commitments within each of the categories were driven in large part by taking into account areas of importance for the company and its stakeholders and also helped form for the structure for internal reporting. According to Kellogg, "Our corporate responsibility strategy has been fully integrated into our business; subject-matter experts for each material area report on progress to the heads of their business units, who, in turn, report up through to a committee of our Board of Directors. In the past two years we have increased incentives for our executives to drive progress in certain corporate responsibility-related areas . . . [and] . . . we worked with our brand leadership teams to help better leverage our corporate responsibility activities in the brands' engagements with consumers."

The "Balanced Scorecard" Approach to CSR Strategy

Traditionally, performance measurement systems relied almost exclusively on management and cost accounting principles, often resulting in an emphasis on short-term results and efficient management of tangible resources (i.e., fixed assets and inventory), which were easier to measure using financial metrics, and failed to pay appropriate attention to non-financial intangible activities (e.g., nurturing of customer relationships, development of innovative products and services, and implementation of high-quality and responsive operating processes) that contributed to the creation of long-term value for the organization. The "balanced score-card" (BSC) perspective was first advanced by Kaplan in the 1980s and is based on the premise that measurement of organizational performance should take into factors that are not purely financial and that organizations should use a management system that is better suited to communicating what they are trying to accomplish; aligning the day-to-day work that everyone is doing with strategy; prioritizing projects, products, and services; and measuring and monitoring progress toward strategic targets. Specifically, the BSC framework is a multidisciplinary view of organizational performance that includes measures such as market share, changes in intangible assets such as patents or human resources skills and abilities (e.g., employee learning and other aspects of so-called organizational capacity), customer satisfaction, product innovation, internal business processes (e.g., productivity and quality), stakeholder performance and potential value of future opportunities that have been created but which have yet to be realized financially.

Proponents of the BSC stress that the term "balanced" is not intended to imply equivalence among the various measures that are used in the framework but rather has been selected to ensure that users of the framework understand that not all key performance metrics are financial and that nonfinancial measures should be considered when looking for ways to improve long-term organizational performance and define and implement the organization's vision, strategy, structure, reporting processes and training, and rewards programs. Not surprisingly, the BSC has been promoted as particularly useful for implementation of CSR initiatives given that the BSC framework explicitly incorporates and balances shareholder, customer, and employee perspectives and can be readily deployed using measurements along three dimensions of performance: economic, social, and environmental. Commentators have suggested that combining the BSC with CSR can and should begin with traditional financial measures and both expand the concept of financial to include CSR-driven market forces (e.g., "green" consumers and energy crunch) and broaden the performance dashboard to include the nonfinancial perspectives associated with the BSC and measured using qualitative and quantitative indicators and targets borrowed from the Global Reporting Initiative's Sustainability Guidelines. This type of approach facilitates identification of new strategic opportunities that also score well in terms of CSR: insisting on supplier performance related to environmental and social commitments can not only improve quality of inputs but also attract and retain new customers that base their buying decisions on trust in the responsible business practices of vendors.

CHAPTER 5

Developing
CSR Commitments

Assessment and strategy development are planning stages in the corporate social responsibility (CSR) process and the real work begins when the company transitions to making its strategy come alive through action. The first step in that process is the development of CSR commitments, which are the policies or instruments that a company develops or signs on to that indicate what it intends to do to address its social and environmental impacts.[1] Hohnen and Potts explained that commitments are essential to the CSR initiative because they ensure that the company's organizational culture is consistent with CSR values; help align and integrate the company's business strategy, objectives, and goals; provide guidance to employees about how they should conduct themselves, which is particularly important for companies whose employees are widely dispersed in locations all around the world; and communicate the company's approach to addressing its societal and environmental impacts to business partners, suppliers, communities, governments, the general public, and others. Commitments can improve the quality of relationships with stakeholders by providing them with reasonable expectations of how the company may behave in a particular situation, thus making the company more transparent and credible and a more reliable business partner. Commitments also provide a basis that senior management and stakeholders can use to benchmark and assess the company's performance with respect to social and environmental responsibility.[2]

---

[1] Hohnen, P., and J. Potts, ed. 2007. *Corporate Social Responsibility: An Implementation Guide for Business*, 42–43, Winnipeg CAN: International Institute for Sustainable Development.
[2] Id. at 42, 44–45.

Development of CSR commitments requires understanding the distinction between aspirational and prescriptive commitments. According to Hohnen and Potts, aspirational commitments typically focus on articulating the long-term goals of the firms with respect to CSR and are usually written in a general language. Aspirational commitments usually take the form of vision, mission, values, and ethics statements and Hohnen and Potts explained that aspirational commitments are intended to articulate a high-level and common understanding of what a company stands for and how it would like to be regarded with respect to its social and environmental positions. Aspirational commitments are important because they offer a basis for a shared view of what the company stands for and where it is heading that can be referenced by people throughout the organization as a guide when the implement the tactics of the CSR initiative. Examples of aspirational commitments include moving to "zero emissions," "eliminating any negative impacts our company has on the environment," and celebrating balanced emphasis on "people, process, product, place and profits."[3]

In contrast, prescriptive commitments, such as codes of conduct and standards, lay out more specific behaviors that to which the company explicitly agrees to comply. Some companies choose to develop their own codes of conduct in order to tailor it to their own specific circumstances; however, this can be a time-consuming process and other companies have found it easier to incorporate and publicly sign on to an existing sectoral CSR code or standard (i.e., codes and standards developed for a particular issue, such as human rights or climate change, or a specific industry, such as mining or agriculture) or another CSR instrument such as the United Nations Global Compact. Many believe that adopting a third-party instrument provides more credibility than relying on a self-developed code, but the codes of conduct of many companies have become recognized standards for excellence and should at least be reviewed before a final decision is made. Third-party instruments allow companies to take advantage of the extensive consultations and discussions among various stakeholders that occurred as they were developed and their adoption signals the seriousness and sophistication of the company's CSR initiative.

---

[3] Id. at 43.

The aspirational commitments typically take the form of a policy statement that articulates the basic values, mission, and goals of the company with respect to CSR and lays out the corresponding targets for the performance of the company against those goals. The policy, which is sometimes referred to as a "commitment statement," should be made available to all stakeholders for viewing on the company's website along with other documents and instruments pertaining to the company's governance and operational guidelines. The responsibility for formulating the policy and selecting the specific objectives or commitments that the company will pursue lies with directors and senior management, all of whom should be visibly involved in the process beginning with stakeholder engagement and continuing through dissemination of the policy and objectives among the stakeholders. The policy statement is generally stated fairly broadly and lays out the company's mission with respect to CSR based on the expectations and needs of all of its stakeholders. The policy statement should be inspirational and should be designed to influence the behavior of management, employees, and other groups such as stakeholders as they go about their day-to-day activities and make decisions about issues relating to the company's overall strategic plan. In other words, the policy statement is an expression of the values upon which the company's business is being conducted and when the policy statement is drafted and adopted by the directors and the members of the senior management team, they are explicitly setting the "tone at the top" of the organization with respect to sustainable development, something that is essential to success of sustainability projects.

In many cases, companies already have some aspirational and prescriptive commitments in place and expansion of the CSR initiative triggers a review and adjustment of existing values, norms, and mission statements, codes of conduct, and compliance procedures. Companies rarely rely on just one of the two types of commitments—aspirational commitments, although relatively general, are an important foundation for the specific tenets in the prescriptive commitments. While adopting third-party CSR instruments appears to be easier and faster than developing a customized code of conduct, senior management must be careful to understand how much work will be needed in order to overhaul the company's operations to the point where it is in compliance with the instrument since it does the company no good to endorse the instrument if it has no reasonable chance to meeting its standards. In particular, senior management should expect that the company will be called upon to benchmark its performance against the standards in the instrument and report the results to stakeholders. In addition, in order for the company's adoption of third-party instruments to be perceived as credible, it will need to participate in third-party verification or certification labeling programs, another expensive and time-consuming process that will sap the company's resources.[4]

Lists of CSR commitments provide a basic framework for the organization's CSR strategy, goals, and objectives and each commitment should have its own set of targets that are defined for a period of three to five years. The organization should also develop a schedule, timetable, and budget for each of the actions associated with the commitments that will be necessary during that period and assign specific personnel to be accountable for seeing that the actions are completed. At this point, the CSR plans should include all of the goals and objectives and the associated indicators. Once an initial list of commitments has been prepared and approved by the top leadership of the organization, they should be reviewed and updated as necessary, no less frequently than annually. Most organizations find it easiest to synchronize their reviews with process of reporting to stakeholders on their CSR activities since they can use the indicators that have been recommended by the sponsors of widely used reporting regimes such as the Global Reporting Initiative (GRI).[5]

Since the development and dissemination of CSR commitments is pivotal to the launch and success of the company's CSR initiative, companies should follow a deliberative process that includes scanning CSR commitments already in use, identifying and understanding existing organizational norms and value, discussions with major stakeholders, identifying the company's key CSR perspectives (i.e., material CSR topics and issues), creation of a working group to develop the list of commitments, preparation of a preliminary draft of the commitments, and identifying and describing

---

[4] Id. at 43.
[5] Id. at 13.

performance targets for the commitments followed by consultation with the affected stakeholders, revision and publication of the commitments and, finally, continuous monitoring of the external environment.[6] It often seems easier to merely adopt, without customization, the standards laid out in recognized third-party CSR instruments; however, doing so misses opportunities to expand organizational understanding of CSR and engage stakeholders in the process in a way that leads to an end product that is focused on their specific needs and expectations and feasible given the company's available resources.

Scanning Existing CSR Commitments

It is useful for members of the leadership team and others involved in the development of CSR commitments for the company to have a good working knowledge of what other companies have done in writing their commitments and the content of third-party CSR codes or standards that the company may elect to adopt. Specifically, a scan should be made of the commitments of comparable firms in the company's business sector, CSR instruments that have been developed by governments in the countries in which the company is currently operating or is contemplating operating in the future, instruments and standards that have been developed by intergovernmental bodies such as the United Nations, and third-party codes and standards that have been developed using international multistakeholder processes (IMPs).[7] While companies generally find many things in the work of others that they would like to include in their own commitments, it is important for the scanning process to be carried out with a critical eye and Hohnen and Potts recommended that

---

[6] Hohnen, P., and J. Potts, ed. 2007. *Corporate Social Responsibility: An Implementation Guide for Business*, 45–46. Winnipeg, Canada: International Institute for Sustainable Development.

[7] Further description and discussion of these models for commitments appears in Gutterman, A. 2019. *Responsible Business: A Guide to Corporate Social Responsibility for Sustainable Entrepreneurs*. Oakland CA: Sustainable Entrepreneurship Project. Available: at www.seproject.org.

the following questions should be asked when reviewing CSR commitments and instruments that were originally developed by others[8]:

- What people and organizations were involved in developing these commitments?
- Would these be the same stakeholders who would need to be involved in the company's own CSR commitments?
- What are the objectives underlying development of these CSR commitments?
- Are those objectives the same as or different from those underlying the company's CSR objectives?
- Can a particular CSR issue identified by the company be resolved or addressed through use of these or similar CSR commitments?
- What are the potential costs, drawbacks, and benefits of the various types of commitments?
- What is the applicability or suitability of these commitments to the organization in light of its scope of activities and geographic range of operations?
- Will the company benefit from the commitments and how?

Companies can, and often do, refer to the issues, criteria, goals, and topics included in what has become a large library of sustainability reporting and standards frameworks. One possibility is the Ceres Roadmap developed and disseminated by Ceres, a nonprofit organization advocating for sustainability leadership (www.ceres.org). The roadmap is intended to be a resource to help companies reengineer themselves to confront and overcome environmental and social challenges and a guide toward corporate sustainability leadership.[9] An important part of the roadmap is the five expectations for performance, which are expressed as "visions" and accompanied by two or more guidelines for achieving those visions. The expectations are described as follows:

---

[8] Hohnen, P., and J. Potts, ed. 2007. *Corporate Social Responsibility: An Implementation Guide for Business*, 46. Winnipeg, Canada: International Institute for Sustainable Development.

[9] Ceres, The Ceres Roadmap for Sustainability (www.ceres.org/ceresroadmap)

- P1—Operations: Companies will invest the necessary resources to achieve environmental neutrality and to demonstrate respect for human rights in their operations. Companies will measure and improve performance related to greenhouse gas (GHG) emissions, energy efficiency, facilities and buildings, water, waste, and human rights.
- P2—Supply Chain: Companies will ensure that suppliers meet the same environmental and social standards—including disclosure of goals and performance metrics—as the company has set for its internal operations.
- P3—Transportation and Logistics: Companies will systematically minimize their environmental impact by enhancing the efficiency of their logistics systems and minimizing associated GHG emissions. Companies will prioritize low-carbon transportation systems and modes, and minimize the carbon footprint of company business travel and commuting.
- P4—Products and Services: Companies will design and deliver products and services aligned with sustainability goals by innovating business models, allocating research and development (R & D) spending, designing for sustainability, communicating the impacts of products and services, reviewing marketing practices and advancing strategic collaborations.
- P5—Employees: Companies will foster a diverse, inclusive, and engaged work environment that holds sustainability considerations as a core part of recruitment, training, and benefits.

As previously noted, each of the performance-related expectations came with specific guidelines that were intended to provide further explanation to companies. For example, the guidelines relating to employees include the following:

- P5.1—Recruitment: Companies will incorporate sustainability criteria into recruitment protocols for all new hires.
- P5.2—Training and Development: Companies will develop and implement formal, and job-specific, training on key sustainability

issues for all executives and employees, and facilitate coaching, mentoring and networks for sustainability knowledge sharing.

- P5.3—Diversity: Companies will build a diverse and inclusive board and workforce. Companies will provide formal diversity training, employee resource groups and advancement opportunities and will identify a senior executive or executive committee with formal responsibility for diversity and inclusion.
- P5.4—Sustainable Lifestyles: Companies will promote sustainable lifestyle choices across their community of employees through education and innovative employee benefit options.

While the Ceres Roadmap is a popular reference point, companies may craft their commitments and goals using the Sustainable Development Goals of the 2030 Agenda for Sustainable Development (commonly referred to as the SDGs), Willard's classification of sustainability-related projects and initiatives based on the Future-Fit Business Benchmark goals and the SDGs, the Global Reporting Initiative, B Lab's Impact Assessment, ISO 26000 Guidance on Social Responsibility, Corporate Knights Global 100, the Sustainability Accounting Standards Board, Integrated Reporting, and/or the United Nations Global Compact.[10] In addition, companies can and should borrow from the work of others while attempting to identify and develop their own sustainability goals and formulate strategies for achieving those goals. As interest in sustainability has grown, companies of all sizes from all parts of the world have published their sustainability goals and provided information on the specific projects and initiatives they have implemented in order to achieve those goals and the metrics they have selected to measure performance and progress toward attainment of the goals.[11]

---

[10] See "Future-Fit Business Benchmark: Mapping of Future-Fit Benchmark Goals to Issues, Criteria, Goals and Topics Included in Other Sustainability Reporting and Standards Frameworks." Available at FutureFitBusiness.org. Several of these standards are discussed in Gutterman, A. 2020. *Sustainability Standards and Instruments*. New York: Business Experts Press.

[11] While CSR leaders can begin by searching for goals published by companies engaged in similar businesses and industries, there are other resources available that facilitate rapid access to publicly available sustainability goals that can be

Organizational Norms and Values

Maignan et al. observed that corporate values play a critical role as a pre-requisite in developing proactive CSR, and that in order to improve organizational fit "a CSR program must align with the values, norms, and mission of the organization."[12] In general, values can be thought of as the ideals and beliefs considered to be core to the company that are used as anchors to guide the behavior of employees and determine all aspects of the way in which the company does business including day-to-day decision making and defining the company's mission and vision.[13] Maon et al. noted that awareness and understanding of the company's vision and values and their relationships to the company's core business practices is crucial and that in order to define or redefine corporate values companies might look at existing credos, corporate charters, mission statements, reports, websites, and other documents.[14]

Once the existing norms have been identified, the next step is to create new norms and values with respect to CSR that incorporate CSR into long-term strategy and decision making, a process that generally involves making a transition from a target-driven culture to a value-driven culture that is receptive to change and capable of sustaining a CSR strategy over the long term. At the same time, companies must develop a better understanding of the objectives, values, demands, and expectations of their stakeholders and make the difficult judgments as to which stakeholders will be given priority when decisions are being made regarding the allocation of the company's scarce resources. Part of this process is engaging

---

used for research, benchmarking, driving performance and accountability. One example is Pivot Goals, which is a database of the sustainability goals of the world's largest and leading companies (http://www.pivotgoals.com/about.php).

[12] Maignan, I., O. Ferrell and L. Ferrell. 2005. "A Stakeholder Model for Implementing Social Responsibility in Marketing." *European Journal of Marketing* 39, nos. 9–10, p. 956.

[13] Maon, F., V. Swaen and A. Lindgreen. 2008. *Mainstreaming the Corporate Responsibility Agenda: A Change Model Grounded in Theory and Practice*, 18. IAG- Louvain School of Management Working Paper.

[14] Id.

with stakeholders to gather their opinions regarding the company's values and planned CSR practices and activities.[15]

Holding Discussions with Major Stakeholders

Developing commitments that align with the expectations of stakeholders and generate enthusiasm for the CSR initiative among those stakeholders requires the active engagement of stakeholders from the beginning of the implementation process. As the company reaches the stage where it is actually preparing the commitments, time should be allocated to hold discussions with major stakeholders. Inside the company, it is crucial to secure the strong support of the board of directors and members of the senior management team to ensure that they provide the necessary "tone at the top" and create incentives that will motivate others in the organization to embrace the CSR initiative. Mid-level managers and frontline employees should also be consulted as they are best positioned to identify practical issues relating to the actual implementation of the plans and policies normally found in CSR initiatives. Current supply chain partners and other important business partners should be consulted in order to gauge how the proposed CSR commitments will impact those relationships. Finally, the company, typically through members of the senior management team, should consult with representatives from consumer, labor, environmental, and community groups. While these consultations typically take the form of discussion with leaders of each of those groups, they should also be expanded to reach the broader members of each constituency. For example, companies often convene consumer focus groups to get feedback on the proposed environmentally driven changes to products and services. Stakeholder consultations may also occur through participation in IMPs, as described earlier.[16]

In many cases the consultation process with the major stakeholders helps the company identify new people outside of the leadership team who are able and willing to make significant contributions to developing

---

[15] Id. at 22.

[16] Hohnen, P., and J. Potts, ed. 2007. *Corporate Social Responsibility: An Implementation Guide for Business*, 46–47. Winnipeg, Canada: International Institute for Sustainable Development.

and implementing the CSR commitments. Where appropriate, these people can be brought into the process by offering them membership on a CSR advisory group that the company establishes as a means for facilitating continuous stakeholder engagement. Hohnen and Potts explained that these groups are generally comprised of experts from the company's key stakeholders, including employees who are continuously engaging with customers and business partners in their day-to-day activities, and are used to review CSR plans, publications, and performance and provide feedback on specific issues.[17]

Among the outcomes of the stakeholder engagement process should be ensuring that the organization's CSR commitments address CSR-related targets for each of the key stakeholders and institutionalizing associated processes such as stakeholder engagement, collaborations with value chain partners, and sustainability reporting and communications. In fact, many companies break out their commitments based on key stakeholder groups. For example, in 2015 Bristol-Myers Squibb described its overall mission to be discovery, development, and delivery of innovative medicines that helped patients prevail over serious diseases and then made the following overall commitment as part of its sustainability report to stakeholders:

> To our patients and customers, employees, global communities, shareholders, environment and other stakeholders, we promise to act on our belief that the priceless ingredient of every product is the integrity of its maker. We operate with effective governance and high standards of ethical behavior. We seek transparency and dialogue with our stakeholders to improve our understanding of their needs. We take our commitment to economic, social and

---

[17] Id. at 47 (citing AccountAbility's "Critical Friends: The emerging role of stakeholder panels in corporate governance, reporting and assurance," 2007 http://www.accountability21.net). Many companies, such as General Electric, have established permanent stakeholder advisory board to provide input into CSR initiatives in specific market sectors (e.g., health) and topics (e.g., supply chain management).

environmental sustainability seriously, and extend this expectation to our partners and suppliers.[18]

Bristol-Myers Squibb then supplemented its overall commitments with a series of specific commitments to each of the stakeholders previously mentioned:

- *Patients and Customers*: We commit to scientific excellence and investment in biopharmaceutical research and development to provide innovative, high-quality medicines that address the unmet medical needs of patients with serious diseases. We apply scientific rigor to produce clinical and economic benefit through medicines that improve patients' lives. We strive to make information about our commercialized medicines widely and readily available.
- *Employees*: We embrace a diverse workforce and inclusive culture. The health, safety, professional development, work–life balance and equitable, respectful treatment of our employees are among our highest priorities.
- *Global Communities*: We promote conscientious citizenship that improves health and promotes sustainability in our communities.
- *Shareholders*: We strive to produce sustained strong performance and shareholder value.
- *Environment*: We encourage the preservation of natural resources and strive to minimize the environmental impact of our operations and products.

Identifying the Company's Key Corporate Responsibility Perspectives

An organization's CSR commitments should be closely aligned to its key CSR perspectives, sometimes referred to as the organization's material CSR issues. Alignment makes it easier for the organization to focus

---

[18] See Bristol-Myers Squibb Sustainability 2015 Goals Final Report.

its attention on a relatively short list of commitments that are easy to describe, such as the following[19]:

- *Employee health and safety:* Ensuring that employees work in a safe environment which meets or exceeds relevant regulatory expectations, addresses health and safety concerns as they arise, and mitigates opportunities for reoccurrence of incidents
- *Product quality and safety to customers:* Choosing materials from quality sources, complying with current "good manufacturing practice," and delivering fit-for-purpose, safe products to customers that adhere to, or exceed strict regulatory standards in all jurisdictions served by the company
- *Corruption and bribery:* Business must be conducted with transparency, and free from unethical persuasion in every aspect of the company's business from identifying product sources, through development of new products, transactions with regulatory bodies, and sale to customers
- *Ethical purchasing and human rights in the supply chain:* Responsibility to partners to ensure our product line is free from human rights concerns such as forced labor and trafficking, unsafe labor standards, and unfair treatment
- *Compliance:* Responsibility to drive compliance with legal and regulatory requirements applicable to our global business including training programs, continuous improvement, and striving for best practices
- *Resource use and waste management:* Reducing the environmental impact of the company's operational activities by managing energy usage during manufacture and logistics, water usage, and waste as a by-product of manufacture
- *Employee development:* Offering employees the opportunity to develop their professional skills mentoring, technical training, and continuing education programs

---

[19] Based on Mayne Pharma Group Limited Sustainability Report 2016, 12, https://maynepharma.com/media/1896/myx_2016_sustainability_report.pdf

- *Making maximum use of new technology:* Developing and acquiring new technologies to improve productivity and operational efficiency in an environmentally and socially responsible manner

Creating a Working Group to Develop Commitments

Once the research has been completed and input has been received from stakeholders, attention turns to developing the initial draft of the CSR commitments. At this point it is helpful to create a working group to handle the drafting responsibilities.[20] Certain members from the leadership team drawn from throughout the organization should be part of the group: board members, senior executives, mid-level managers, and frontline employees. In addition, however, it is important to bring people from outside the leadership team into the process including people who are skeptical about the value of the initiative and representatives of the stakeholder groups that will be most impacted by the commitments given the CSR strategy upon which the commitments will be based. For example, it is very important to encourage employees to make suggestions and creative methods for soliciting input should be considered (e.g., facilitated brainstorming sessions that focus on creating a "future vision" of the company once CSR initiatives are in place). All the members should commit in advance to actively participating and check their schedules and other priorities to be sure that they will be able to devote the necessary time and resources to the project. A working group manager or chairperson should be selected to facilitate communications and ground rules should be set by the entire group at its first meeting regarding the group's objectives; members' responsibilities; anticipated workload, and outcomes; the ground rules on how the group will operate; and the extent of reliance on any of the external CSR instruments described earlier.

---

[20] The discussion of ISPs in this paragraph is adapted from Hohnen, P., and J. Potts, ed. 2007. *Corporate Social Responsibility: An Implementation Guide for Business*, 47. Winnipeg, Canada: International Institute for Sustainable Development.

As discussed in the following, the working group will be responsible for drafting the company's CSR commitments and the drafting process will require referencing the efforts of other companies and international references as a potential foundation for the company's documents. Since there are literally hundreds of CSR-related codes and standards already in place, the working group needs to establish a procedure for monitoring developments relating to intergovernmental commitments and nongovernmental or private sector codes and creating a library of references that can be consulted. Larger organizations may even consider joining an existing instrument that is recognized by their stakeholders as reputable and actively participating in ongoing discussions that ultimately lead to revisions of the instrument. This approach is a good way to demonstrate to stakeholders that the company is engaged as a leader in setting appropriate standards and also provides an opportunity for the company to be privy to new trends and developments so that it can be among the first to address them in its own commitments.

Preparing a Preliminary Draft

The working group should prepare a preliminary draft of the CSR commitments that can be circulated for review and comment by all affected parties.[21] While one or more persons from the working group should have lead responsibility for preparing the draft, they should involve others in the organization who are not members of the working group to be sure that there is input from those who will be involved in the actual implementation of the commitments. While the commitments should be customized to the company's particular situation, it is recommended that the drafters use existing CSR instruments as base documents in order to have a better idea of what should go into the commitments and how the elements should be organized and described. As mentioned earlier, the universe of potential models is daunting and the working group should focus on instruments that are consistent with the company's goals, values,

---

[21] The discussion in this paragraph is adapted from Hohnen, P., and J. Potts, ed. 2007. *Corporate Social Responsibility: An Implementation Guide for Business*, 51. Winnipeg, Canada: International Institute for Sustainable Development.

and, most importantly, identified current CSR strengths, weaknesses and priorities.

The preliminary draft should generally include a statement of the company's commitment to CSR and make it clear that all employees, consultants, and suppliers are expected to comply. Topics to be covered generally parallel those included in well-known international instruments and might include human rights, the environment, health and safety, competition, improper payments, workplace harassment and shareholders, media, and community relations. It is also common to include a general statement and definition of the company's core values such as integrity, accountability, and transparency. The commitments document should illustrate how each of these values is to be integrated into the expected actions of each of the covered groups in relation to the various topics mentioned previously. Companies should avoid "niche," or narrowly drawn, commitments and define them broadly in order to have more opportunities to make an impact and engage with a larger audience. Some companies are interested in pursuing political causes; however, politics often divides more than it unifies and may not be the best choice of commitment. In addition, commitments need to have a long shelf-life and this means that commitments tied to a single person or brand should be avoided since there is too much risk of something happening that causes the person or brand to fall out of favor.

The preliminary draft should be reviewed and approved by the working group and then distributed and explained to members of the board of directors and senior management team since all of them will be important players in discussing the commitments with stakeholders. Whatever commitments are selected, they must generate passion throughout the company and among the company's stakeholders. They cannot simply be an "add on" to the business, and they must be authentic and embedded in the core of the company's brand and culture. If this does not happen, then the company will derive no value from its sustainability initiatives and consumers and other potential critics in a world connected by social media will quickly sense the possibility of "green washing" and the company's reputation will suffer dramatically. Internal review also provides an opportunity to identify and assess actions and investments that will be needed to support the commitments such as modifications of the company's brand guidelines and corporate identity; displaying the mission broadly on the company's website, in press releases, and in marketing materials; developing ways to empower employees to become engaged in the mission such as creating volunteer programs and distributing information about the mission to employees to ensure that they are aware of what the company is doing and that they understand the importance of the mission and their support of the mission; creating and executing opportunities to demonstrate the commitments in visible ways such as donating cash, hosting a fundraising event, or having a team of employees volunteer at an organization engaged in activities related to the commitments; and developing partnerships with other organizations, as well as individuals, involved in supporting the same commitments.

Commitments are generally not the place for additional details regarding the strategies that will need to be implemented to fulfill the commitments, particularly since the strategies will necessarily change as time goes by and priorities change among the entire portfolio of sustainability commitments. Some companies will, however, mention actions that will be taken that are reasonably related to eventually establishing specific goals and targets for each of the commitments. For example, companies may include intentions in their commitments relating to undertaking assessments of environmental risks, establishing formal environmental protection programs, establishing assurance programs, preparing and publicly disseminating sustainability reports, providing training programs to employees and suppliers, and developing and implementing new product design and packaging programs.

Identifying and Describing Performance Targets for Commitments

When developing CSR commitments, attention needs to be paid to defining and expressing in measurable terms the target level for its performance with respect to each of the commitments, since the company and the interested stakeholders will need to track performance with respect to each of the commitments and related goals. When setting the targets, consideration should be given to both effectively managing material risks to the business and meeting expectations of key stakeholders. The initial target level depends on the current status of the company's CSR activities and companies should expect to periodically review and, as appropriate, reset the targets. At a minimum, companies need to comply with all laws and regulations applicable to their business operations; however, a serious CSR effort goes beyond minimum compliance to include both surpassing the requirements of laws and regulations and making and keeping voluntary sustainability commitments selected by the company that are related to the company's key CSR matters. The next level is meeting the expectations of markets and stakeholders, which inevitably exceeds legal and regulatory compliance and can be understood only through a process of extensive engagement with investors and other key stakeholders. Finally, some companies may progress with the CSR to the point where they become recognized as being among the pioneers of CSR and create best practices.[22]

Fairly obvious cases where specific metrics are included in what are otherwise high-level commitments include the target percentage for reduction of packaging waste, injury and illness rates among employees, energy and water use, and greenhouse gas emissions. Providing continous communication to and training for employees is a more difficult proposition; however, companies can easily address this topic by establishing formal programs that ensure that employees have access to necessary information and that they are actually attending classes and completing certification programs to demonstrate that they have understood and absorbed the information. For larger businesses, it will be necessary to determine the appropriate level of aggregation. For example, the initial objective or goal may be to reduce waste at all of the company's locations by a specified percentage; however, the situation at each location will likely be different and the attainable reduction at some locations may be less than the overall goal while other locations will be able to exceed the overall goal.[23]

[22] 2016. *Finnish Textile and Fashion Corporate Responsibility Manual*, 13. Helsinki: Finnish Textile and Fashion.

[23] The specific goal for each location will be set out in detailed commitments and goals for that location and a secondary measure of performance, apart from the overall objective for waste reduction companywide, might be what percentage of the locations achieved their specific goal.

When drafting and reviewing its commitments and related goals, the company should of course consider whether they are actually attainable and consistent with the company's business strategies and core competencies. In the ideal situation, the commitments and objectives will follow naturally from the strategic goals that the company has already established using traditional profit-focused principles and the performance measures for the objectives can simply be added to the existing key performance indicators (KPIs). The more likely scenario, however, is that the company will find that existing strategies are not sufficient to achieve the sustainable development objectives and/or in conflict with those objectives. In either case, the directors and senior management may have to revisit the company's economic strategies and modify them before releasing a finished list of sustainable development objectives. The most common example of this is the need to adjust return on investment goals to account for the short-term costs of implementing technologies and processes necessary to achieve the environmental targets.

Consultation, Revision, and Publication

Once the preliminary draft has been circulated internally and approved for wider distribution, the next step is to engage in consultations with the persons and stakeholder groups who will be impacted by the implementation of the commitments.[24] The goal of these consultations is to explain how prior input from stakeholders has been incorporated into the draft and inform stakeholders who have not been directly involved up to this point about what the company is considering. While working group members should develop and monitor a consultation plan, members of the senior management team should expect to be heavily involved at this stage as they are best situated to communicate and explain the commitments and vouch for the company's intentions and resources for fulfilling the commitments. Feedback from these consultations should be delivered to the working group and appropriate changes should be

---

[24] The discussion in this paragraph is adapted from Hohnen, P., and J. Potts, ed. 2007. *Corporate Social Responsibility: An Implementation Guide for Business*, 52. Winnipeg CAN: International Institute for Sustainable Development.

made to the commitment document to generate a final draft that can be "published" by distribution to employees, posting on the company's website, and through other appropriate communication techniques to ensure that impacted stakeholders are aware that the commitments are in place. Before the commitments are published, appropriate changes should be made to other organizational charter documents (e.g., mission statement, statement of values, and codes of ethics and conduct) to integrate the new CSR commitments. In addition, before external publication, the company should carefully map out how the commitments will be implemented, a process that is described in more detail as follows, and plans should be in place to begin engaging with employees and other stakeholders on how the commitments will be work in practice (e.g., training sessions for employees, planning meetings with supply chain members, and other key business partners and "town halls" with community groups).

Communications About Commitments and Performance

Since continuous internal communication about CSR commitments increases awareness of CSR, Maon et al. argued that companies implementing CSR commitments should develop an internal communication plan that identifies and uses various means of communication such as newsletters, magazines, annual reports, meetings, and training.[25] The focus of the communications will vary depending on the stage in the implementation process. For example, at the beginning, communications will include reports on the changes that are going to be made and seek to reassure employees by informing them on the program's progress as well as on misconceptions in relation to the CSR implementation process. These types of communications should be designed in way that will elicit feedback from throughout the organization on the effects of the implementation process and assist top management in its efforts to clearly identify and delineate role relationships and expectations. As the implementation

---

[25] Maon, F., V. Swaen and A. Lindgreen. 2008. *Mainstreaming the Corporate Responsibility Agenda: A Change Model Grounded in Theory and Practice*, 32. IAG- Louvain School of Management Working Paper.

process moves forward and the CSR commitments become more embedded in organizational culture, communications will shift toward publiciz-
ing and demonstrating the success of the CSR program and anchoring
the CSR vision in the day-to-day activities of the organization.[26]

As for external communications regarding CSR, Maon et al. noted
that organizations should be ready to communicate externally what has
already been realized and what is still to achieve, but that decisions regarding the nature and the level of communication about CSR practices are
complex and the need to communicate about CSR commitments varies
according to stakeholders, the importance they put on CSR issues, and
the potential harmful impact and influence of the stakeholders on the
concerned organization. As such, careful identification and prioritization
of stakeholders as well as continuous dialog with stakeholders regarding
their needs and expectations relating to CSR-related issues is essential
to creating an effective external communications program.[27] As for planning for the communications program itself, consideration should be
given to establishing brand and messages, developing communications,
and outreach tools (e.g., a dedicated page on the organization's website,
e-newsletters, and other outreach materials tailored to the requirements
of specific stakeholder groups), securing media coverage for key events
and initiatives, designing and implementing stakeholder education campaigns, and strategies for facilitating communications by other supporters
of the organization's CSR programs and initiatives (e.g., politicians and
community leaders).[28]

Continuous Monitoring of the External Environment

At the same time the company is debating and selecting its initial CSR
commitments, it should also be setting up a monitoring system that
assists the directors and members of the senior management team to keep

---

[26] Id. (citing Klein, S. 1996. "A Management Communication Strategy for
Change." *Journal of Organizational Change Management* 9, no. 2, p. 33.
[27] Id. at 35.
[28] Wolk, A., and K. Kreitz. 2008. *Business Planning for Enduring Social Impact.*
Cambridge MA: Root. Appendix D: Project My Time Phase One Action Plan—
Communications Section.

abreast of developments that may impact the content and/or implementation of the commitments. Among other things, the monitoring system should be robust enough to include new and proposed legislation; emergence of, or modifications to, industry practices and standards; strategies and practices of competitors; activities, policies, and concerns of community and special interest group policies; where applicable, concerns of trade unions; and development relating to technologies that have, or may have, an impact on the activities of the company and/or those of the company's stakeholders. In the past, monitoring focusing on CSR topics has often been delegated to an environmental and/or social issues committee or group that then reports back in to the directors and senior managers; however, if CSR is really going to be at the core of the company's overall mission, the external scanning associated with it should be fully integrated into its strategic management processes.

The external monitoring process should not be viewed as a passive collection of information but rather as an opportunity for the company and its leaders and employees to proactively engage in debates relating to formulation of CSR policies and practices. Companies can get involved in the activities of industry associations relating to sustainable development and work with legislators and special interest groups on relevant laws and regulations. In fact, while the government has stepped in to set legal and regulatory guidelines with respect to various CSR and sustainability topics, much of the standardization to date has come from the efforts of NGOs and industry groups that promulgated their own standards with input from the same stakeholders that the company is engaged with on its own objectives. Setting standards that are widely recognized and acceptance is a difficult process; however, if the efforts are successful the company can benefit from having clearer guidelines against which internal goals can be established and stakeholder reporting can be based. One example of industry standards that illustrates how companies can work together to significantly improve all of their processes and the overall well-being of their stakeholders is the "Responsible Care" initiative launched in the chemical industry.

CHAPTER 6

Implementing
CSR Commitments

Companies often announce their corporate social responsibility (CSR) mission statements and commitments with great public fanfare, pledging to proactively contribute to improving social conditions and protecting the environment. While putting the company's brand and reputation on the line in this way is important, the reality is that CSR cannot and will not be effective unless and until it is tightly integrated into every aspect of organizational operations including products and services, governance systems and practices, culture, marketing and other external communications, training, recruiting, and relationships with business partners. Once the CSR commitments are finalized and published, attention needs to be paid to the actual implementation of those commitments, which includes the day-to-day decisions, processes, practices, and activities that are required in order for the company to adhere to its commitments and effectively carry out its overall CSR strategy. A company that fails to implement its CSR commitments will find itself losing employees, customers, and business partners and will see its standing in the marketplace and community plummet.

There is no universal approach to implementing CSR commitments and the methods used by companies will vary depending upon the specific content and focus of their commitments, current organizational structure, organizational culture, resources, priorities of the CEO, and the other members of the senior management team and other factors. One way to view the process is as follows: develop a CSR implementation plan; establish an internal organizational structure; implement CSR management systems; develop a sustainability-oriented organizational culture; develop an integrated CSR decision-making structure; prepare and implement a CSR business plan; set measurable targets and identify performance measures; integrate CSR into strategic values; engage employees and others to whom CSR commitments apply; design and conduct CSR training; establish mechanisms for addressing problematic behavior; create internal and external communications plans; and implement CSR partnering arrangements. While primary responsibility for CSR implementation may be vested with a group or department, input and support will be need from the board of directors, all members of the executive team and managers and employees in all of the functional and customer departments. Also important to effective CSR implementation is continuously building stakeholder awareness through messaging and engagement. While most of the issues relating to the actual implementation of the CSR strategy come into play once the strategic plan is finalized, it is important for those involved in the preparation of the strategy to identify and resolve the practical problems that are likely to arise when actual pursuit of the goals and objectives begins.

Developing a CSR Implementation Plan

As the company goes through the process of identifying, vetting, and approving the CSR objectives and commitments, attention also needs to be paid to translating the policy and the accompanying objectives into operational terms, a process that requires the development of an implementation plan. The plan will be expansive and will impact the entire organization including corporate culture and employee attitudes; organizational design and structure, particularly the responsibilities and accountability of everyone in the organization with respect to the CSR objectives and commitments; information reporting systems; management systems, and operational practices. During the planning process, the objectives and commitments will necessarily remain fluid since they should not be finalized and announced to the world unless and until the company has a clear and reasonable plan for implementation.

As the plan develops consultations with stakeholders will be needed and ideas from stakeholders should be solicited about how best to realize their needs and expectations. While all stakeholders are important, input and participation from employees is essential since they will be the one called upon to implement the plans and will likely feel significant disruption to the ways in which they have worked in the past. The input from stakeholders will likely cause a series of modifications to the plan as well as to the upper tier goals and objectives. Eventually the plan will be ready for review and approval by the board of directors following presentation by the senior management at the same time that the board signs off on the policy and related objectives and commitments. Given the breadth of the organizational changes that will likely be required, it should be expected that the implementation plan will cover three to five years and provide for milestones that will hopefully be achieved every six to twelve months.

Before an effective and reasonable implementation plan can be prepared, the company needs to know where it stands with respect to how its activities in their current state line up against broadly accepted sustainable development principles and the needs and expectations of its stakeholders. Insights must come from the assessment process describe elsewhere in this publication that covers the company's overall strategy and its operational activities, management philosophies and systems, relations with stakeholders, and the functionality of the information systems that will be relied upon to generate the data about CSR performance that must be reviewed by company leaders and reported to stakeholders. At the assessment stage, the company can rely on questionnaires that have been prepared by industry groups and outside organizations such as the Global Environmental Management Initiative and Ceres and bring in outside consultants that can help facilitate the process.

The results of the assessment need to be put into context by comparing them to the status and performance of comparable organizations as well as industry standards and norms and expectations that have been established by external groups. Comparisons can be made through a review of public disclosures by comparable organizations and data compiled by industry associations and programs that have been formed explicitly to collect and catalogue CSR information. Comparison allows the company to identify the gaps between what it is doing and what others are doing and provides a sense of the reasonable targets that the company can establish for improving its CSR profile. The senior management of the company should create a set of goals and objectives and a strategy, timetable and milestones for each goal and objective. The strategy should not only be approved by the board of directors, it should also be fully vetted by all of the key players inside the organization to ensure that they have had a chance to contribute to the process and can "buy in" to the strategy because they have participated in its formulation and believe in its objectives.

While the board of directors and senior management will retain ultimate responsibility for the success of the company's CSR goals and objectives, responsibility for overseeing and tracking the company's progress toward the goals and objectives should be assigned to a specific group within the organizational structure that is provided with the resources and authority required to discharge its duties. When creating the strategy and the accompany implementation plan, the following steps and issues should always be part of the process[1]:

- The job descriptions of everyone in the organization, managers and employees, should be reviewed and revised to integrate specific CSR roles, responsibilities, and accountability. Everyone needs to know their place in the plan and to whom they are expected to report.
- Changes to the organizational culture will be required, as will retraining of employees to empower them to carry out their new roles and responsibilities. As part of this process, reward systems and incentives will also need to assessed and modified to align with the activities required to achieve the CSR objectives and commitments. It is also likely that new skills and experience will need to be added to the workforce and the human resources department will need to understand the needs of the company and set up new recruiting initiatives.
- Changes to the strategic planning processes should already have begun as the CSR objectives and commitments were being developed; however, at the implementation stage, an investment must

---

[1] *Business Strategy for Sustainable Development: Leadership and Accountability for the 90s.* 1992. Winnipeg, Canada: International Institute for Sustainable Development.

be made in the resources and skills necessary to handle stakeholder engagement and external monitoring.

- Each of the CSR objectives and commitments will have their own
  unique set of metrics, most of which will be new to the company,
  and this means that the company's management information systems will need to be changed in order to ensure that everyone has
  access to the information they need in order to be sure they are on
  track with the new metrics and see their progress toward achieving the objectives and commitments.

- The company's marketing research efforts will need to be over-
  hauled to place customer attitudes and expectations regarding
  CSR and sustainability front and center. While customers as a
  group will be consulted during the stakeholder engagement process, detailed market research, including interviews and tests, will
  be needed to determine the best way to position the company's
  CSR initiative and the related features in its products and services.
  The results of this research should be reflected in updated plans
  with respect to pricing, sales, marketing, and promotion. Companies often find that existing markets will need to be redefined and
  that new markets should be added.

- The engineering and product design groups will need to determine what changes must and can be made to products and processes in order to achieve the CSR objectives and commitments
  and satisfy the needs and expectations of the company's stakeholders. The company should not commit publicly to a specific
  leap in the energy efficiency of its products until it is satisfied
  that progress can be made in a manner that does not endanger
  the company's ability to survive financially or adversely impact
  another group of stakeholders (e.g., displacing a large number
  of workers). Specific consideration should be given to regulatory
  requirements, industry standards, and benchmarking.

- Suppliers are key partners in any company's efforts with respect
  to CSR and other stakeholders, such as customers and human
  rights activists, will hold companies accountable for the social
  responsibility (or lack thereof) of their suppliers. This means that
  everyone involved in the procurement process must be trained in

supply chain management and held accountable for the products procured from vendors and the manner in which those products are produced.

- The CSR objectives and commitments cannot be realized unless the company remains profitable throughout the process and is able to survive and thrive to the point where the objectives have been achieved. As such, the implementation plan must be supported by comprehensive financial planning that takes into account and addresses all of the capital requirements that must be satisfied in order for the plan to be successful including making sure that capital required for investment in new technologies and other resources will be available at the appropriate times during the three- to five-year span of the plan. Among the issues to be considered is the impact of the sustainability focus on attracting capital from outside investors and the availability of tax incentives and financing through governmental programs.

The process of creating a CSR implementation plan is extremely challenging and will require a thorough understanding of the tools associated with organizational design. In addition to the afore-described issues, senior management needs to be acutely aware of potential barriers and sources of resistance to the changes that will be needed in order to implement the plan effectively. The transition toward a stronger focus on CSR will inevitably upset people in the organization who prefer that things continue as they have always been and individuals and groups will be reluctant to embrace change and agree to new roles and reporting channels. As such, it is essential that senior management involve everyone in the organization in the planning process and refrain from finalizing the plan until those who will be responsible for executing the plan have had a chance to voice their concerns and ask about the uncertainties that are bothering them.

Establishing Internal Organizational Structure

One of the first steps in integrating CSR is to ensure that the board of directors is "on board" with the initiative. An important way that the board can demonstrate its support is to ensure that the company has an effective internal organizational structure for its CSR and sustainability activities. Many companies are creating an additional position among the members of the senior executive team that is specifically focused on corporate sustainability. Appointing these "chief sustainability officers" (CSOs) not only demonstrates a high level of commitment to the area by the directors and also helps everyone inside and outside the company to identify the person who will likely be the company's spokesperson on corporate sustainability issues and responsible for managing the resources provided by the board to implement sustainability strategies and satisfy the company's disclosure obligations. The CSO must be prepared to support the board as it considers CSR and corporate sustainability issues, engage with the company's stakeholders, and, not unimportantly, effectively coordinate the efforts of all of the various departments within the company that should be involved in sustainability initiatives (e.g., investor relations, legal, operating heads, and risk management).[2]

Heidrick and Struggles created a list of necessary competencies for an effective CSO, beginning with the ability to think strategically, which was described as the ability to look toward the horizon, identify an opportunity or challenge before it affects the company, and develop and implement a strategy to either take advantage of the opportunity or manage the challenge. Particular attention was given to the creation of business opportunities by the CSO, a marked shift from focusing primarily on prevention, mitigation, and compliance. For example, the CSO can proactively seek out technological solutions to environmental problems that simultaneously reduce costs and improve productivity, a true "shared value" proposition. A second key competency for the CSO identified by Heidrick and Struggles was the ability to communicate effectively and translate complex technical concepts and strategies into terms that resonated with the company's top leadership and key constituencies (i.e., employees, investors, lenders, insurers, rating agencies, customers, suppliers, the media, and the public). When communicating, the CSO needed

---

[2] Kuprionis, D., and P. Styles. September/October 2017. "Translating Sustainability into a Language Your Board Understands." *The Corporate Governance Advisor* 25, no. 5, 13–16.

to be able to adapt his or her tone and approach to a wide range of audiences ranging from the CEO, directors, and regulators to each of the employees who would be called upon to change their skills and behaviors in order to execute the sustainability strategy.[3]

Implementing CSR Management Systems

Like any other strategic initiative, CSR must be managed effectively. As such, CSR implementation should include plans for designing and operating a CSR management system that incorporates each of the company's strategic CSR topics and includes all of impacted tasks within the company's value chain. One company organized its CSR-related activities by reference to four themes: internal controls, human resource management, environment management, and social contribution. Internal controls included the actions of the board of directors and executive team to oversee the company's CSR programs through the implementation of a transparent corporate governance system that built and maintained trust among all of the company's stakeholders. Two other important areas of internal control included compliance with laws, internal regulations, and corporate ethics, thereby including not only formal laws and regulations but also voluntary standards adopted by the company including codes of conduct and procedures relating to CSR-related activities and transactions such as workplace safety and conflicts of interest; and risk analysis and management to ensure the safety of employees, customers, and other stakeholders and reduce and prevent losses of business resources. With respect to human resource management, the company committed itself to respecting the creativity and personality of each and every employee and to valuing a corporate culture that enabled its diverse human resources to fully display their knowledge and capabilities. Environmental management activities focused on reducing the negative impacts on the environment generated by the company's operational activities. As for social contribution, the goal of the company was to contribute to local communities in ways that leveraged the company's unique characteristics in order to improve the quality of life in those communities and provide

---

[3] Id. at 9.

opportunities for personal development. The efficacy and performance of the CSR management system against industry standards need to be continuously assessed through external evaluations by third-party organizations, a requirement frequently imposed by customers of the company, and internal audits conducted by a dedicated group within the company established to promote and support CSR activities and staffed with certified personnel trained in the audit standards of industry associations.

Researchers on corporate sustainability from the *MIT Sloan Management Review* and the Boston Consulting Group (BCG) urged companies to embed sustainability organizationally through cross-functional teams, clear targets, and key performance indicators, and reported that building sustainability into business units doubled an organization's chance of profiting from its sustainability activities.[4] The report provided insights into how BASF SE, the large German chemicals company, organized its "accelerator" approach to sustainability.[5] An important element was "top-down" engagement that began with creation of a sustainability board that was chaired by a member of the board of directors and included leaders from each of the company's business lines. The board then pushed all of the company's business units from a "middle-out" perspective to rigorously assess all of their products against strict sustainability criteria. Products that did not meet the requirements for "accelerator" status fell into one of three other categories: "performer" products that met basic market standards, "transitioners" products that were actively addressing sustainability issues, and "challenged" products that carried significant sustainability risks. Product teams for products in any of these categories were charged with developing plans to improve their standing on the scale; however, care was taken to ensure that leaders of each of the business units were informed about the goals and purposes of the sustainability board to secure their buy-in to what would almost certainly be a significant disruption to preexisting business practices at the company. Once the sustainability board had collected information from each of the business

---

[4] Kiron, D., G. Unruh, N. Kruschwitz, M. Reeves, H. Rubel, and A.M. zum Felde. 2017. "Corporate Sustainability at a Crossroads: Progress Toward Our Common Future in Uncertain Times." *MIT Sloan Management Review*, 11.
[5] Id.

units, it returned to the entire board to present its findings and secure a mandate from the directors to implement the accelerators program as a comprehensive sustainability solutions approach to reimaging each of the company's product lines. The drafters of the report argued that identifying business and sustainability risks within business units allowed BASF to create market solutions that would not have happened otherwise.[6]

Effective implementation of the strategic plan requires careful attention to scheduling and establishing control systems. In order for the implementation process to be effective, and for the company to be able to quickly make any needed corrections, a small group of senior managers should be given the task of directing, coordinating, and reviewing the planning process. This group must be held accountable for making sure that the action plans are carried out. In fact, for growing companies, the process of planning and attempting to implement the plan is almost as important in and of itself even if the plan fails or must be changed. In any event, the coordination team should establish a schedule of regular meetings to review the progress of the plan against performance targets. This schedule can be used as the basis for setting deadlines for collection of information from the coordinators for each plan.

Developing a Sustainability-Oriented Organizational Culture

It is clear that over the last several decades organizations have continuously expanded the application of the principles of sustainable development to the business world and that companies have increasingly focused efforts on introducing or changing policies, products, and/or processes to address pollution, minimize resource use, and to improve community and stakeholder relations.[7] However, while these initiatives are laudable,

---

[6] The accelerators program also included essential stakeholder communications such as providing members of the sales team with product cards that described each product's sustainable characteristics in order to ensure that the message of each product's sustainability benefits reached customers. Id.

[7] Linnenluecke, M., and A. Griffiths. 2000. "Corporate Sustainability and Organizational Culture." *Journal of World Business* 45, 357 (citing Crane, A. 2000. "Corporate Greening as Amoralization." *Organization Studies* 21, no. 4, 673.

some critics have argued that they are often largely superficial and not conducive to the creation and maintenance of authentically sustainable organizations and industries.[8] For them, the only way that an organization can truly and fully respond to environmental and social challenges and become sustainable is to undergo a significant cultural change and transformation that leads to the development and maintenance of a sustainability-oriented organizational culture.[9] In fact, studies have indicated that there is a strong relationship between organizational culture and corporate sustainability and that sustainability initiatives are more likely to be successful if they are defined and implemented in a way that is aligned with the organizational culture.[10]

Bertels prepared a report that was distributed through the Network for Business Sustainability (NBS) that proposed a framework for embedding sustainability in organizational culture that was designed for executives and senior human resources and sustainability managers and also

---

[8] See, for example, Hart, S. and M. Milstein. 2001. "Creating Sustainable Value." *Academy of Management Executive* 17, no. 2, 56; and Senge, P., and G. Carstedt. 2001. "Innovating Our Way to the Next Industrial Revolution." *MIT Sloan Management Review* 42, no. 2, 24.

[9] Crane, A. 1995. "Rhetoric and Reality in the Greening of Organizational Culture." *Greener Management International* 12, 49; Post, J., and B. Altman. 1994. "Managing the Environmental Change Process: Barriers and Opportunities." *Journal of Organizational Change Management* 7, no. 4, 64; and Stead, W., and J. Stead. 1992. *Management for a Small Planet: Strategic Decision Making and the Environment.* Newberry Park, CA: Sage. (as cited in Linnenluecke, M., and A. Griffiths. 1992. "Corporate Sustainability and Organizational Culture." *Journal of World Business* 45, 357.)

[10] Tatarusanu, M., A Onea and A. Cuza. 2020. "Organizational Culture and Values for Corporate Sustainability." University of Iasi, http://docplayer.net/11003116-Organizational-culture-and-values-for-corporate-sustainability.html (accessed May 1, 2020). See also Abbett, L., A. Coldham and R. Whisnant. 2020. "Organizational Culture and the Success of Corporate Sustainability Initiatives: An Empirical Analysis using the Competing Values Framework." https://researchgate.net/publication/282195341_Organizational_Culture_and_the_Success_of_Corporate_Sustainability_Initiatives_An_Empirical_Analysis_using_the_Competing_Values_Framework (if there is greater congruence between organizational culture and the sustainability initiative, the initiative will be more successful, and the greater the congruence the greater the success of the initiative).

included a portfolio of 59 practices that had either been shown to be effective by research or that showed potential but remained untested.[11] The framework grouped the practices into four different categories: fostering commitment; clarifying expectations; building momentum for change; and instilling capacity for change. Bertels and the NBS recommended that sustainability leaders employ a selection of practices from each of the framework's four categories, thus creating a change program that simultaneously included practices for delivering on the organization's current sustainability commitments, affecting values and behaviors inside the organization, establishing rules and procedures that could be followed by organizational members to advance sustainability initiatives, and moving the organization further along the path to sustainability.

The NBS also collaborated with Canadian Business for Social Responsibility (CBSR) on a workshop involving sustainability and human resources professionals that involved the exchange of information on best practices for embedding sustainability into organizational culture. The workshop led to the creation of a framework that was based on the five elements of organizational design in the well-known "Star Model" developed and popularized by Galbraith and included strategic planning (e.g., incorporating sustainability into mission and vision statements), organizational structure (e.g., creating an executive position with responsibility for sustainability), human resource management (e.g., providing sustainability training to employees), processes (e.g., collecting and reporting data on sustainability performance), and employee rewards and incentives (e.g., incorporating sustainability into financial and nonfinancial rewards programs). This framework included certain "best practices

---

[11] Bertels, S. 2010. *Embedding Sustainability in Organizational Culture: A How-to Guide for Executives*. London, Ontario CN: Network for Business Sustainability. A longer version of the report, which includes more discussion of academic research, including 179 studies conducted over fifteen years, and detailed information on the practices discussed in this section (including case studies), was published as Bertels, S. 2010. *Embedding Sustainability in Organizational Culture: A Systematic Review of the Body of Knowledge*. London, Ontario CN: Network for Business Sustainability. and is available for downloading at http://nbs.net/knowledge/topic-culture/culture/systematic-review/ (accessed May 1, 2020).

for embedding sustainability in organization culture," which are briefly described in the following paragraphs.[12]

Eccles et al. observed that even though there was empirical support for the view that adoption of sustainability-related strategies was necessary in order for companies to be competitive and that "high sustainability" companies significantly outperformed counterparts that had not adopted environmental and social policies, relatively few companies exhibited a broad-based commitment to sustainability on the basis of their original corporate DNA.[13] Because of this Eccles et al. argued that most companies needed to make a conscious and continuing effort to formulate and execute a sustainable strategy and embed sustainability into their strategy and operations. Based on their research comparing the organizational models of "sustainable" and "traditional" companies, they concluded that companies needed to be prepared to embark on large-scale change in two stages: the first stage involves reframing the company's identity through leadership commitment and external engagement, and the second stage involves building internal support for the new identity through employee engagement and creating and codifying mechanisms for execution.[14]

Eccles et al. argued that the first stage in becoming a sustainability company—reframing the company's identity—requires both leadership commitment and external engagement. Transformation of the company's organizational culture requires the strong and focused guidance of the leadership team and the organizational leaders are the people who are best situated to drive the necessary engagement relating to sustainability between the company and the diverse range of external stakeholders

---

[12] Network for Business Sustainability and Canadian Business for Social Responsibility, Embedding Sustainability in Organizational Culture: Framework and Best Practices. For further discussion of the "Star Model," see A. Gutterman: Organizational Design: Creating an Effective Design for Your Business (Oakland CA: Sustainable Entrepreneurship Project, 2019) available at www.seproject.org. See also Galbraith, J. 1977. *Organization Design.* Reading, MA: Addison-Wesley.
[13] Eccles, R., K. Perkins and G. Serafeim. Summer 2012. "How to Become a Sustainable Company." *MIT Sloan Management Review* 53, no. 4, 43–44.
[14] See "About the Research" on page 45 in the article for an extended discussion of the methodology used by the researchers and the scope of the companies surveyed.

including investors, community members, regulators, activists, and members and representatives of civil society. The goal at this stage is to strengthen the commitment to sustainability at the top of the organization and redefine the company's identity to the world as being an organization that has embraced the principles of sustainability and embedded them in its organizational culture, strategy, operational processes, and relations with stakeholders. As the organizational leaders begin to reach out to external stakeholders, they gather the information necessary to formulate and execute the company's sustainability strategy. As the engagement process expands in the second stage to include employees their interaction with external stakeholders creates opportunities for learning that can be used to make the company more innovative and committed to creating value for itself and society in general. Leadership commitment and external engagement should continue during the second stage of the process as parallel drivers of the company's new identity.

The second stage of the process of creating a sustainable company involves building internal support for the new identity developed during the first stage through employee engagement and creating and codifying mechanisms for execution. Eccles et al. defined employee engagement as the actions that the company takes in order to secure the interest and attention of its employees in the company's sustainability efforts and the roles that employees are asked to play. In most cases, the transition to become a sustainable company will require that employees change their behaviors and behavioral change will not occur unless the employees believe that it will be worth it. Employees will also need to understand and accept the reasons for the company's decision to make changes and have a clear picture of the specific individual role that they are expected to play and how their performance will be measured. The process of employee engagement will not be easy; however, Eccles et al. pointed out that engaged employees are emotionally connected to their work and to their workplace and thus tend to be more productive and more willing to engage in discretionary efforts to achieve company goals.[15]

---

[15] Id. at 47.

Developing an Integrated CSR Decision-Making Structure

Hohnen and Potts noted that the first question that needs to be answered when the time comes to implement CSR commitments is "given the firm's existing mission, size, sector, culture, way of organizing its affairs, operations and risk areas—and given its CSR strategy and commitments—what is the most effective and efficient CSR decision making structure to put in place?"[16] They argued that since CSR is fundamentally concerned with transparency, accountability, and performance, the decision-making structure for CSR must be an integral component of the company's governance activities that is visible to all impacted parties, accountable throughout the organization, supported by coordinated cross-functional decision making and specialized staff expertise, and designed in a way that it can easily be verified both internally and externally.

Given the importance of senior level support and enthusiasm for the CSR initiative, it is not surprising that people and committees at the top level of the organizational structure will be tapped for CSR leadership roles and decision-making responsibilities. Active involvement and oversight by the board of directors is critical to the success of any CSR initiative. The board is ultimately responsible for the actions of the managers of the company and for reviewing and approval the company's overall strategic including its sustainable development policies, objectives, and commitments. While all of the members of the board have the same duties in this area, it is common to create a committee of the board, often called the "social responsibility committee," that will include members that will focus their attention on setting corporate policies on CSR and for dealing with issues such as health and safety, personnel policies, environmental protection, and codes of business conduct. The committee will be the first line of review at the board level for the strategies and implementation plans relating to CSR proposed by senior management and, once those strategies and plans are approved by the entire board, the committee must monitor implementation by receiving regular reports

---

[16] Id. at 58.

from throughout the organization. The committee must also ensure that the strategies and plans are implemented consistently, which is particularly challenging when the operational activities of the company are disbursed over many locations and/or the company is heavily dependent on third parties for activities, products, and services. Any CSR board committee should have its own charter and procedures, reviewed and approved by the entire board. In addition, time should be set aside during each meeting of the directors for the entire board to focus on progress toward CSR commitments and hear reports from key CSR decision makers throughout the organization, since even though some CSR responsibilities may be delegated in some manner that each of the members of the board should understand that CSR has been added to all of their duties and must be considered in any decisions that may be made in the boardroom.

Operational responsibility for overseeing and tracking the company's progress toward its CSR objectives and commitments should be assigned to a specific department or group within the organizational structure. Just below the board level, a senior executive should be appointed to manage overall CSR implementation throughout the company. The CSR executive should either be a full member of the company's "C-suite" or report directly to the CEO and, as necessary, to the board of directors. In many cases, the CSR executive will be supported by a CSR implementation committee that includes representatives from key departments or business units that are most impacted by the CSR initiative and who will report to the CSR executive. For example, Hohnen and Potts suggested that the implementation committee would normally include representatives from environmental, health and safety protection, worker relations, supplier relations, community relations, and customer relations. It needs to be clear to committee members that their service is valued and important to the company and appropriate changes should be made to their job descriptions and the criteria that will be used to evaluate their performance and set their compensation and other incentives. The implementation committee should also be supported by specialists in important areas such as stakeholder engagement and monitoring of environmental changes impacting sustainability, including legislation and reporting.

The discussion so far presumes a relatively centralized structure for managing the CSR initiative; however, how it works in actual practice depends on the balance that is struck between reserving decisions for the CSR implementation committee and allowing individuals, departments, and business units to decide on the best way to implement the CSR commitments given the specific context in which they operate. For example, some companies create CSR committees within each of the existing business units (e.g., functional, product, and/or market) and those committees focus on the plans relevant to their units. Organizational culture and management style plays a big role in deciding between centralization and decentralization; however, regardless of the path the company takes, it is important for every employee to understand how they are expected to contribute to the CSR initiative.[17] The decision-making structure should also be designed with an eye toward anticipating the inevitable conflicts that employees will encounter when satisfying requirements for social and environmental responsibility appear to conflict with striving for the highest levels of economic performance.

Ideally companies will be able and willing to make all of the changes to their organizational structure that is reasonably necessary to align their chain of authority and collaborative activities with the CSR commitments. In many cases, however, this is not practical and CSR duties and responsibilities will be added to the preexisting activities of various departments such as human resources, environmental practices, health and safety, legal, and community affairs. While this is a good first step, there is a risk that the new duties will overwhelm existing resources and it will also take time for each of these departments to properly integrate CSR into their overall business and operational plans. Companies should strive to create independent CSR departments or groups that are self-sustaining and include people and other resources whose primary responsibility is

---

[17] Some companies use a hybrid approach and a matrix reporting structure that includes both a CSR executive (and supporting group) and business unit committees and requires managers and employees to report both to their unit leaders and the CSR executive.

CSR. Hohnen and Potts suggest that these groups can focus on simple cost-saving or revenue-enhancing initiatives such as energy savings, waste reduction, and employee and customer loyalty programs. The groups can provide the overall planning and oversight and engage other departments as necessary. In this way, the company can begin getting used to considering CSR in all of its activities and the group can help other departments understand how their participation in CSR can actually improve their performance.[18]

Preparing and Implementing a CSR Business Plan

The responsible members on the board of directors, the CSR executive, and other senior personnel with important decision-making responsibilities relative to CSR should develop an actual CSR business plan, which can be a separate document or incorporated into the company's overall business plan. The CSR business plan should track the CSR strategy and commitments that have previously been approved and should identify all of the human, financial, and other resources and activities that will be necessary in order to effectively implement the CSR commitments and track company performance in meeting those commitments.

The business plan is also an opportunity to lay out specific plans and tactics for each of the key CSR commitments. For example, Hohmen and Potts suggested that a basic plan for meeting a commitment that prohibits illegal bribes to government officials might include the following elements:

- Establish appropriate training for all employees who have regular contact with government officials during the course of their day-to-day job activities. The course should focus on the distinction between proper and improper payments, with an online version that includes "frequently asked questions" that can be consulted when questions arise.

_____

[18] Hohnen, P., and J. Potts, ed. 2007. *Corporate Social Responsibility: An Implementation Guide for Business*, 65. Winnipeg, Canada: International Institute for Sustainable Development.

- Review the company's incentive and disincentive structure (e.g., commissions) to ensure it does not indirectly encourage improper behavior. In other words, employees should not feel additional pressure to "close deals" that causes them to consider offering bribes to government officials who are in a position to influence decisions.
- Set up a procedure for seeking and obtain advice on payment issues. For example, the company should designate a member of the legal or compliance department to field payments questions and set up a "hotline" that employees can use to seek advice and/or report improper behavior.
- Create "whistleblower" protection measures that remove concerns among employees that they will be retaliated against if they report information relating to an actual or potential improper payment.

Each of the actions in the CSR business plan should be assigned a schedule and timeline and the resource requirements for each action should also be laid out in advance. It should go without saying that the company should not make a public commitment to a CSR activity unless it is willing to invest sufficient resources to effectively pursue and achieve the goals associated with the activity. Whenever the plan calls for assigning new duties and responsibilities to managers and employees, appropriate changes should be made to their job descriptions, reporting requirements, and performance objectives.[19] While the basic elements of a CSR business plan apply to all companies, the size and scope of operations of the company obviously need to be taken into account. Small businesses will certainly not have the resources available to large global organizations and their CSR business plans should be scaled appropriately since they generally will not be able to hire new staff and set up dedicated CSR departments. In general, small businesses should begin with a single CSR project that excites managers and employees and which can be reasonable integrated into their existing duties and responsibilities.

---

[19] For further discussion of business plan preparation, see Gutterman, A. 2019. *Strategic Planning and Business Plan Preparation: A Manager's Guide.* Oakland CA: Sustainable Entrepreneurship Project. Available: www.seproject.org.

In addition to a business plan for the organization's overall sustainability strategy, business plans should be created for each specific program or initiative in order to focus the organization on the steps that will need to be taken in order for the program or initiative to have the desired environmental or social impact. When preparing such a business plan, attention should be paid to carefully describing the specific environmental or social problem or need and the opportunities that the organization has identified for not only alleviating the problem but also making an innovative positive net impact on the organization's business and the stakeholders most affected by the problem. The business plan should include an overview of the environmental or social problem that includes current trends, root causes, and an assessment of the relevant factors in the economic, environmental, social, cultural, and political environments. Attention should be paid to the barriers that have previously prevented effective resolution of the problem, a discussion which should serve as an opening to explain the organization's views as to opportunities that have been missed.[20]

Setting Measurable Targets and Identifying Performance Measures

Internal management control, as well as the ability to create and disseminate external reports, depends on developing appropriate means for measuring performance and assessing the resulting metrics against internal and external performance standards. Implementing and managing corporate responsibility is no different than any other strategic initiative: measurable goals must be established, results must be measured and assessed, and new goals must be continuously set based on ongoing stakeholder analysis, evolving risks, and SWOT analysis. While the financial performance of companies has long been measured using an array of national and international standards for the preparation of financial statements and the accounting profession has developed a robust set of rules and

---

[20] Wolk, A., and K. Kreitz. 2008. *Business Planning for Enduring Social Impact.* Cambridge MA: Root Cause. Appendix B: Outline of a Business Plan for Enduring Social Impact.

guidelines to ensure the comparability and clarity of those statements, the definition and presentation of performance indicators for corporate responsibility is an evolving art and science.

Implementation of the CSR program will require upgrade to the company's information systems to ensure that they are capable of supporting the creation of the reports needed by management and external stakeholders. The information that is required, and the type of performance that will be measured and reported, will vary depending on the specific CSR commitments and objectives. Governmental and public agencies, as well as other participants in the industry in which the company is operating, play an important role in establishing standards and identifying the expected performance targets. For example, it is commonplace for companies to track and report emission levels and/or working hours lost due to illness or accident and the measuring procedures of the company should be set up in a way that tracks those metrics accurately and facilitates comparisons to internal targets and the performance of comparable companies. While companies may already be tracking the appropriate information, it is common to find that new measurement procedures will need to be introduced. In addition, while governments often take the lead from industry practices in establishing regulatory standards, the measurement requirements eventually adopted by regulators may be different and this will require companies to continuously update their measurement and management systems (this is one reason why it is recommended that companies proactively engage with regulators as they set their standards to promote consistency and settle on standards that meet the needs of both the public and business).[21]

External standards, measures, and reporting systems often take a significant time to develop and gain acceptance and companies often need to make their own decisions about the best way to measure performance for their specific CSR objectives and commitments. In those situations, the goal should be a cost-effective solution that simultaneously meets the needs of managers and the applicable external stakeholders. While

---

[21] Hohnen, P., and J. Potts, ed. 2007. *Corporate Social Responsibility: An Implementation Guide for Business*. Winnipeg, Canada: International Institute for Sustainable Development.

the CSR business plan is being prepared, the drafters need to identify appropriate and measurable goals for each of the commitments in order to track progress and determine if changes are needed to the plans or the commitments themselves. Hohnen and Potts noted that measuring success required identifying the objectives underlying a CSR commitment, developing key performance indicators, working out the measurement method, and measuring the results.[22] When setting targets an effort should be made to keep them simple, measurable, achievable, reliable and time-bound.

Companies generally use a mix of qualitative and quantitative performance measures. For example, quantitative measures might include tracking the amount of waste sent to landfill when the commitment relates to reduction of solid waste or the number of local community or stakeholder meetings when the commitment is improving communications with community and stakeholder groups. Quantitative measures include assessing feedback from customers and other stakeholders on the value and effectiveness of particular CSR actions done in furtherance of commitments. Many commitments require both quantitative and qualitative measures: when assessing improvement of community relations, both the number of community meetings and attendee satisfaction with those meetings needs to be considered. As a practical matter, the most meaningful measures of performance are those that are focused on demonstrable impact with respect to a given environmental or social issue.

However, as more companies have committed to voluntary sustainability reporting and organizations such as the Global Reporting Initiative (GRI) have gained traction as standards setters for appropriate indicators of environmental and social performance, companies are able to use those indicators as a basis for their responsible management efforts. Specifically, companies can refer to indicators included the GRI reporting framework that cover each of the major topics and concerns of responsible management including financial responsibility, environmental responsibility, responsibility toward personnel, collaboration with partners, and product

---

[22] Id. at 59–60.

responsibility as well as related areas such as community engagement and investment.[23]

The GRI reporting framework is extensive and designed to meet the needs of a wide range of companies of varying sizes that are operating in different sectors. No single company can or should afford the same weight and attention to each indicator, instead the task associated with reporting as part of responsible management is to identify those indicators that are most relevant and material to stakeholders' understanding of the company's corporate responsibility performance. While indicators can be integrated after the company has completed the stakeholder engagement and risk and SWOT analysis, it is useful to consult the reporting frameworks in advance as they can provide ideas that can be used in the initial corporate responsibility analysis and to help the company focus its attention and resources. All of the indicators should be reviewed, weighted, and prioritized, with initial rankings discussed with stakeholders to ensure that they reflect the stakeholders' main concerns and expectations regarding reporting. Reference should be made to indicators selected by competitors so that the company's reporting can be easily compared to others in the same market.

The reporting frameworks are used primarily to present information on the company's corporate responsibility performance with respect to its own operational activities; however, the framework also provides guidance on information that should be collected from partners in the production chain for the company's products in order to provide readers of the finished report with an understanding of the corporate responsibility management conducted by those partners and the impact that it has on goods and services that their company produces. For example, if a number of the company's products incorporate components developed and manufactured by outside vendors and/or are manufactured on an outsourced basis, the picture of the environmental and social footprint associated with those products is not complete without an understanding of how corporate responsibility is managed among the suppliers and manufacturers that the company relies upon. A company that practices

---

[23] 2016. *Finnish Textile and Fashion Corporate Responsibility Manual*, 25–26. Helsinki: Finnish Textile and Fashion.

high standards of corporate responsibility management internally yet knowingly or negligently countenances actions by the supply chain partners that harm the environment and/or disrespect the human rights of their workers must be held accountable, and for many companies the greatest corporate responsibility risks (and opportunities) can be found in their supply chains.

While often discussed separately, corporate responsibility indicators and reporting should be considered throughout the process of stakeholder engagement and analysis, risk analysis, and SWOT analysis. Establishing the focus of the company's corporate responsibility activities and the associated management processes requires input from key stakeholders and provision should be made for giving each of them ample opportunity to participate in the process. Through stakeholder engagement, the company can improve its understanding of the risks that the company faces and can often tap into the ideas provided by stakeholders to develop business opportunities. As noted earlier, companies do not have to report on all of the indicators included in the GRI framework and should be most attentive to those indicators that are material; however, the reporting can and should be tailored to all of the issues that are most important to the company's unique set of stakeholder interests and expectations. Companies also need to remember that while reporting should reflect performance against various quantitative and qualitative indicators, it is also an opportunity for the company to describe its process of engagement and analysis, the way the company is applying its strengths to address threats and exploit opportunities and the steps that the company is taking in order to strengthen weaknesses in its business model that are preventing it from achieving better corporate responsibility success and while may ultimately expand into substantive risks for the business.

It is important to understand that meeting a performance target does not necessarily mean that there has been satisfactory progress toward achieving success with the related commitment. Hohnen and Potts pointed out that even if the company dramatically increases the number of meetings with community members relations with the community will not necessarily improve if those meetings do not address the problems and concerns raised by the community. In that situation, the tactics need to be changed in order for progress to be made. For example, more resources may need to be placed into investigating and resolving specific complaints, a process that plays out outside of the public meetings. A properly crafted commitment and performance target should not only include metrics on the number and types of community engagements but also objective feedback on community satisfaction with the company's initiatives for engagement and involving community groups in decision making.

Another thing to consider when setting goals and performance targets for commitments that are primarily grounded in social and environmental areas is the potential impact on the economic performance of the company. For example, as noted by Hohnen and Potts, reducing emissions can actually increase the company's profitability, although it may take time to actually see a reduction in energy costs that exceeds the initial investment in the emission reduction efforts (this is one reason why emission reduction goals and targets should be framed within an extended time period). In addition, the public commitment to reducing emissions and otherwise acting in an eco-friendly manner will hopefully improve the reputation of the company's brand and open opportunities to do business with new customers motivated to work with environmentally responsible companies. In the same vein, targeting measurable improvements in the supply chain will likely make the company a more attractive potential partner for retailers and other business partners looking to improve their own supply chain management profile.

Engaging Employees and Others to Whom CSR Commitments Apply

Responsibility for the implementation of the CSR commitments falls heavily on the shoulders of employees and it is essential to have them involved in the process of developing the commitments and provide them with the tools and incentives to be vigorous champions of CSR in their dealings with customers, suppliers, community members, and other stakeholders. If employees are not effectively engaged in the CSR initiative, the company will find that other stakeholders lose confidence in the company's dedication to CSR and will find the company's written CSR commitments to be little more than words on paper.

Hohnen and Potts recommend that employee engagement should begin by making sure that employees are aware of CSR directions, strategies, and commitments, hopefully building on their involvement in earlier activities in the implementation process.[24] Employees need to hear directly from senior management of the company about the reasons that the CSR commitments have been adopted, why they are relevant to the goals and future of the company and how they will likely change the way that the company operates. Most importantly, each employees needs to have an understanding of his or her role in implementing the CSR commitments and the issues and considerations that he or she should consider whenever a decision is made or an action is to be taken. Hohnen and Potts suggested that companies can build and maintain employee support for CSR implementation by taking the following steps:

- Providing early and intensive training about the CSR initiative to key decision makers and influencers so that they can champion the commitments and proactively introduce the concepts of CSR in their day-to-day interactions with their colleagues;
- Incorporating CSR performance elements into job descriptions and performance evaluations for positions at all levels of the organization;
- Providing regular updates on progress in meetings or the company newsletter and using other internal communication strategies subsequently discussed;
- Developing incentives (e.g., monetary and other rewards for best suggestions);
- Removing or reducing disincentives (e.g., competing interests such as premature deadlines that encourage employees to choose non-CSR options);
- Offering incentives and recognition for good ideas; and

---

[24] Hohnen, P., and J. Potts, ed. 2007. *Corporate Social Responsibility: An Implementation Guide for Business*, 61–62. Winnipeg, Canada: International Institute for Sustainable Development.

- Making it a practice to celebrate CSR achievements in order to motivate and inspire employees to continue pursuing the CSR initiatives.

In order for employees to feel engaged in the CSR implementation process and carry out their new duties and responsibilities, they need to be adequately and continuously trained. Employee training is essential for any CSR program to be effective. It is not sufficient to adopt formal policies and procedures if employees do not understand what is expected of them and the reasons for the CSR initiatives. Training sessions should be held at the time the CSR initiative is about to be launched in order to orient employees about their roles and teach them the specific skills and competencies they require. Training should continue in the months and years that follow as commitments and circumstances change and the company begins to address new CSR issues and develops new CSR programs. Ongoing training is also a good opportunity to efficiently share best practices throughout the organization.

Creating Internal and External Communications Plans

Plans should be created to ensure that information regarding the company's CSR commitments, activities, and performance is widely and continuously communicated both inside the company and to the company's external stakeholders. Communications regarding CSR activities and the results of those activities should be conducted using a wide range of channels such as the company's website and newsletters to the company's customers. Companies should also collaborate with value chain partners and other stakeholders on communications planning and execution and should participate in events related to CSR as a means for gathering information and raising awareness of the company's involvement. While much of the communication activity relates to disseminating the results of the CSR initiatives and programs, dialogue with stakeholders should begin early in the process so that stakeholders can provide inputs into the company's decisions regarding CSR commitments and areas of focus.[25]

Internal Communications

An important part of strengthening employee engagement in CSR is making sure that they have current information and companies use a number of methods including newsletters, annual reports, Intranet communication, meetings, and training. Communications reinforces that CSR is a priority within the organization and also provides employees with the tools they need to discuss the CSR initiative and commitments among themselves and with customers, suppliers, and business partners. Managers and supervisors should be required to put CSR topics on the agenda for all internal group meetings in order to provide employees with an opportunity to share stories or ideas.

With respect to communications, it is essential that every employee understand the company's mission statement and related goals and objectives and, as mentioned earlier, the preferred approach to developing the plan in the first place is to solicit the opinions of all the employee groups who are essential to successful implementation of the plan. If the employees understand and accept the goals and objectives established by senior management they are more likely to accept instructions and conscientiously carry out their duties and responsibilities. Moreover, they will be motivated to contribute to effective execution of the strategy and make suggestion about how to make necessary projects flow more smoothly.

Communications can include the distribution of information about plans, business operations, competitors, and the overall business environment in which the company operates, and can take the form of meetings, written reports, newsletters, leaflets, informal conversations during the workday, and multimedia presentations. In addition to their role in educating employees, communications can also provide a basis for collecting feedback from throughout the organization and motivating employees to

---

[25] Hohnen, P., and J. Potts. 2007. *Corporate Social Responsibility: An Implementation Guide for Business*, 64. Winnipeg, Canada: International Institute for Sustainable Development.

pursue higher performance objectives that they have had a hand in setting. Finally, communication skills can be used to develop trusting relationships between managers and employees, particularly when managers are communicating with employees regarding his or her performance.

Managers must be mindful of the different channels of communication that normally coexist in any company. For example, vertical communication, which usually goes up and down the organizational structure through formal reporting procedures, is the way that managers communicate assignment, feedback on prior performance, and information about the company to subordinates. In turn, subordinates use vertical communication channels to deliver requests and suggestions as well as responses to communications that have previously been delivered from above, often in the form of reports. In contrast, horizontal communications are those that occur among and between managers and other employees at the same general level in the organizational hierarchy. Using written reports and meetings, horizontal communications generally focus on coordination of responses to vertical communications from above and on building teams and groups across various organizational lines.

Managers should, and often do, spend significant amounts of time on creating and improving formal communication systems within the company. For example, it is important to have systems in place that will provide managers with regular reports on the status of the selected control points in the organizational structure. In addition, formal feedback methods, including suggestions systems and questionnaires, are a good way to begin to institutionalize a more participatory and decentralized style of management. However, managers should also not overlook the importance of informal communications. Managers should look for opportunities to mingle with employees at their workstations and can useful informal meetings as an opportunity to gauge the acceptability of ideas that the manager might be considering for formal implementation.

Some of the problems that might arise during the communication process include the following:

- Avoidance and lack of opportunities for face-to-face communications can lead to misunderstandings as messages get garbled and confused as they pass through a long line of intermediaries.

- Prejudice or distrust among the communicators can also hamper communications, since the participants either lack respect for the other party or feel that the communication is not reliable.
- Communications are often made to the wrong audience which means that the proper recipients here the information from an inappropriate source and often receive it in an inaccurate form.
- Senior managers sometimes deliver directives to subordinates in a disrespectful, often humiliating fashion, thereby creating an unpleasant environment for understanding the actual communication.
- Communications may be less effective because managers fail to include all responsible parties in the original delivery of the message, such as when a meeting is held without all the necessary personnel.
- Communication pessimism, and frustration, can arise from the failure of a party to participate in a timely dialogue on important issues, as happens when suggestions or requests go unanswered or unacknowledged for lengthy periods of time.

Managers must carefully examine their organizations with an eye toward identifying any of the potential communications problems listed earlier, or other factors that may lead to situations where it is clear that important messages and information are not understood. The next task is to devise and implement effective solutions to these problems, including scheduling of meetings with opportunities for questions and discussion of directives and ideas, team building, regular and timely reports of performance, and other information that are generally and consistently available to all employees, and suggestion systems. In some cases, managers may implement training programs focusing on communications skills, not only for managers but also for others throughout the organization. Training should cover a variety of skills, including listening, writing, conducting meetings, public speaking, and negotiating.

Managers must also make an effort to prepare to make communications that are effective, accurate, timely, and directed to the proper audience. This requires careful planning of meetings and other presentations and make sure that the information is packaged in a way that is meaningful to the audience. When discussing problems, the manager should also be prepared to describe solutions or secure feedback from the audience if the purpose of the presentation is brainstorming or collection of suggestions. Finally, choice of media is important, with sensitive matters best handled verbally with appropriate written follow-up if necessary.

External Communications

As noted during the discussion of developing CSR commitments, a key step in CSR implementation is making the company's CSR commitments "public." Many companies place their CSR commitments on their websites and on packaging for their products and this is important to making those commitments credible and real to stakeholders; however, these are only the first steps and companies need to have an external communications plan that focuses on individuals and groups outside of the company that need to be aware of the CSR initiatives and the company's progress toward achieving its commitments. Among other things, companies should prepare list of persons and groups who should be formally notified of the CSR commitments and receive copies of the documents with a personal note from a company executive. In addition, companies conduct awareness campaigns that include advertising, speeches and other media events and community meetings. Web site references to CSR can and should be expanded as time goes by to include more information, reports and case studies of the company's CSR activities. Investor relations strategies should be modified to incorporate CSR strategies.

CHAPTER 7

Measuring Planning Performance and Effectiveness

Regardless of the specific strategic planning processes for corporate social responsibility (CSR) initiatives, companies must be sure that they create adequate controls so that activities carried out in furtherance of the strategic, tactical, and operational plans can be monitored and evaluated. This serves several important purposes including making sure that the plans and their associated activities are being executed properly and on a timely basis and that adjustments can be made as necessary in order to remedy weaknesses in the original plans and/or adapt to unforeseen changes in the company's business environment. Attempts to measure strategic planning effectiveness had traditionally been limited to using financial criteria that provide a scorecard of the financial performance of the company; however, new approaches to assessing organizational results and performance adopted over the last few decades had expanded the notion of strategic planning effectiveness to include many other nonfinancial, qualitative criteria associated with core business process, customers, employees, organizational learning and innovation, and other core areas in the companies important for the overall organizational performance.[1] For example, companies can now choose from among a wide range of new tools including activity-based management, value-based

---

[1] B. Sukle and S. Debarliev, "Strategic Planning Effectiveness: Comparative Analysis of the Macedonian Context." *Economic and Business Review*, 14(1) (2012), 63, 66.

management, the balanced scorecard, "benchmarking," and customer relationship management.[2]

Wolk et al. argued that performance measurement provides vital information for advancing social innovation, which they defined as the process of developing, testing, and honing new and potentially transformative approaches to existing social issues.[3] They believed that having the right performance metrics, data, and analysis in hand allowed social innovators (i.e., nonprofit organizations, government agencies, and businesses that offer innovative, results-driven solutions to social problems) to make well-informed management decisions to drive continuous improvement and long-term social impact and answer the following fundamental questions[4]:

- How do we know how well our organization is progressing against our mission and goals?
- What should we measure in order to have critical information without becoming overwhelmed with data?
- How should we report and discuss our performance internally among staff and board members to maximize learning?
- Where should we focus our organization's limited resources in order to increase our effectiveness today and achieve sustainability over the longer term?
- How can we most effectively measure and communicate our performance and impact to external stakeholders?

Wolk et al. advocated for the adoption of a performance measurement system as a means for organizations to efficiently collect and make use of data about their activities (i.e., programs, services, and initiatives run by the organization) and operations (i.e., human resources management, technology, financial management, governance etc.). From their

---

[2] L. Digman, *Strategic Management: Competing in a Global Information Age* (Mason, OH: Thomson Learning, 2002).

[3] Wolk, A., A. Dholakia, and K. Kreitz, *Building a Performance Measurement System: Using Data to Accelerate Social Impact* (Cambridge, MA: Root Cause, 2009), iii.

[4] Id. at 3–4.

perspective, a performance measurement system constituted a cycle that included four major phases of activity[5]:

- *Measure:* Organizations operating performance measurement systems use indicators, metrics that are tracked regularly, to assess their activities and supporting operations.
- *Report:* Organizations can use several types of reporting tools to compile performance measurement data into a format that is easy to analyze including a dashboard, which includes a focused selection of indicators to provide periodic snapshots of the organization's overall progress in relation to past results and future goals, and/or a report card, which contains highlights from an organization's internal dashboards and facilitates sharing data externally with social impact investors and other stakeholders.
- *Learn:* Using the selected reporting tools, an organization's leadership and other key staff members review and interpret performance data in order to make well-informed decisions and identify opportunities for improvement and necessary course corrections.
- *Improve:* The organization implements its decisions to improve its activities and operations and the performance measurement cycle begins again.

Development, implementation, and continuous refinement of the performance measurement system mentioned previously includes various steps such as planning; choosing what to measure (e.g., indicators of organizational health, CSR program performance, and social and economic impact) and how to do it; creating processes, such as dashboards, for using the data in day-to-day decisions, performance reviews and overall strategic planning; and auditing the measurement process and related systems to ensure it is working and identify improvements that might be necessary to remediate reporting issues and generate even more useful data. Attention to the performance measurement system should not be delayed until the end of the strategic planning process. In fact, when weighing and selecting CSR commitments, the members of the leadership team must

---

[5] Id. at 6.

consider whether it will be feasible to measure progress toward a particular commitment and generate sufficient data to transparently report on the company's performance. If something cannot be measured, it will not get done, and attempting to explain a commitment that lack clear metrics and targets will only cause confusion among stakeholders and create skepticism about the company's CSR strategies and skills.[6]

Reporting and Verification

In order to know whether or not the CSR initiative and its related commitments are actually improving the company's performance, it is necessary to have in place procedures for reporting and verification, each of which are important tools for measuring change and communicating those changes to the company's stakeholders.[7] Hohnen and Potts described reporting as "communicating with stakeholders about a firm's economic, environmental and social management and performance" and verification, which is often referred to as "assurance," as a form of measurement that involves on-site inspections and review of management systems to determine levels of conformity to particular criteria set out in codes and standards to which the company may have agreed to adhere.[8] Verification procedures should be tailored to the company's organizational culture and the specific elements of the company's CSR strategy and commitments; however, it is common for companies to rely on internal audits, industry (i.e., peer) and stakeholder reviews and professional third-party audits. Verification procedures should be established before a

---

[6] Wolk et al. also included a "Performance Measurement Audit Tool" as Appendix A to their publication as a resource for use in conducting the performance measurement audit. Id. at 60–62.

[7] For detailed discussion of sustainability reporting, see A. Gutterman, *Sustainability Reporting and Communications* (New York, Business Experts Press, 2020), available at www.seproject.org.

[8] P. Hohnen (Author) and J. Potts (Editor), *Corporate Social Responsibility: An Implementation Guide for Business* (Winnipeg, Canada: International Institute for Sustainable Development, 2007), 67.

specific CSR initiative is undertaken and should be included in the business case for the initiative.[9]

One basic reason for reporting and verification is to make sure that the CSR initiative is properly managed and that persons involved understand they will be accountable for their actions. Other good reasons for reporting and verification include giving interested parties the information they need in order to make decisions about purchasing the company's products and/or investing in the company (the level of funding from investors focusing their interest on ethical businesses is continuously increasing) or otherwise supporting the company's community activities; collecting information that can be used to make changes and improvements to the company's CSR strategy and commitments; improving internal operations; managing and reducing risks; and strengthening relationships with stakeholders. However, in order to achieve the greatest benefits from reporting and verification companies need to carry out those activities in a rigorous and professional manner using tools and standards that are widely recognized and accepted among those interested in the results.

The scope of the company's reporting and verification efforts will depend on various factors including the size of the company, the stage of development and focus of its CSR commitments, legal requirements, the financial and human resources available for investment in those activities and the degree to which companies want and are able to integrate sustainability indicators into their traditional reporting of financial results. Ceres, a nonprofit organization advocating for sustainability leadership (www.ceres.org), has developed and disseminated its Ceres Roadmap as a resource to help companies reengineer themselves to confront and overcome environmental and social challenges and as a guide toward corporate sustainability leadership.[10] In the area of disclosure and reporting, Ceres stated that the overall vision was that companies would report regularly on their sustainability strategy and performance, and that disclosure

---

[9] Companies using the Future-Fit business goals recommended by the Future-Fit Business Network can adopt the "fitness criteria" associated with each of the goals. See the discussion of the Future-Fit business goals elsewhere in this Guide and Future-Fit Business Framework, Part 1: Concepts, Principals and Goals (Future-Fit Foundation, Release 1, May 2016), 25, FutureFitBusiness.org.

[10] Ceres, The Ceres Roadmap for Sustainability (www.ceres.org/ceresroadmap)

would include credible, standardized, independently verified metrics encompassing all material stakeholder concerns, and details of goals and plans for future action. Specific expectations regarding disclosure were as follows:

- D1—Standards for Disclosure: Companies will disclose all relevant sustainability information using the Global Reporting Initiative ("GRI") Guidelines as well as additional sector-relevant indicators.
- D2—Disclosure in Financial Filings: Companies will disclose material sustainability risks and opportunities, as well as performance data, in financial filings.
- D3—Scope and Content: Companies will regularly disclose trended performance data and targets relating to global direct operations, subsidiaries, joint ventures, products, and supply chains. Companies will demonstrate integration of sustainability into business systems and decision making, and disclosure will be balanced, covering challenges as well as positive impacts.
- D4—Vehicles for Disclosure: Companies will release sustainability information through a range of disclosure vehicles including sustainability reports, annual reports, financial filings, corporate websites, investor communications, and social media.
- D5—Verification and Assurance: Companies will verify key sustainability performance data to ensure valid results and will have their disclosures reviewed by an independent, credible third party.

The ISO 26000 Guidance on Social Responsibility developed and released by the International Organization for Standardization noted that reporting to stakeholders could be done in many different ways, including meetings with stakeholders, letters describing the organization's activities related to social responsibility for a defined period, website information and periodic social responsibility reports (either stand-alone or as part of the organization's annual report with financial information).[11] Since the primary audience for the reporting is the stakeholders, the organization should provide information on how and when stakeholders have been involved in the design and implementation of the reporting process. Additional considerations relating to reporting cited in ISO 26000 included[12]:

- The scope and scale of an organization's report should be appropriate for the size and nature of the organization.
- The level of detail may reflect the extent of the organization's experience with such reporting (i.e., limited reports covering only a few aspects may be provided when the CSR initiative is first launched and coverage can be expanded as time goes by and the organization has more reporting experience).
- The report should describe how the organization decided upon the issues to be covered and the way those issues would be addressed and should explain how the choice of issues is responsive to the needs and expectations of stakeholders.
- The report should present the organization's goals, operational performance, products and services in the context of sustainable development.
- The presentation in the report about performance on social responsibility should be comparable both over time and with reports produced by peer organizations, recognizing that the nature of the report will depend on the type, size, and capacity of the organization.

---

[11] ISO 26000 Guidance on Social Responsibility: Discovering ISO 26000 (International Organization for Standardization, 2014) and Handbook for Implementers of ISO 26000, Global Guidance Standard on Social Responsibility by Small and Medium Sized Businesses (Middlebury VT: ECOLOGIA, 2011). ISO 26000 is available for purchase from ISO webstore at the ISO website (www.iso.org) and general information about ISO 26000 can be obtained at www.iso.org/sr.

[12] ISO 26000 Guidance on Social Responsibility (Geneva: International Organization for Standardization, 2010), 78–80.

- A brief explanation should be provided as to why topics omitted from reports are not covered to show that the organization has made an effort to cover all significant matters.
- The report should be supported by a rigorous and responsible process of verification, in which the data and information are traced back to a reliable source to verify accuracy of that data and information.
- The reporting content and process should conform to the reporting guidelines of an external organization.

Reporting regarding CSR and sustainability will only be valuable if the information that is provided by the organization is perceived to be truthful, accurate, and balanced. In other words, organizations should strive to enhance their credibility regarding their CSR through stakeholder engagement and dialogue including involving stakeholders in the process of verifying the organization's claims regarding its CSR performance. In Section 7.6.1 of ISO 26000, it is recommended that organizations make arrangements with their stakeholders to allow them to periodically review or otherwise monitor aspects of an organization's performance. Credibility can also be improved by participation in specific certification schemes that may touch on a range of CSR issues such as product safety and environmental impact and labor practices. In addition, organizations can build trust in their CSR reporting by establishing advisory boards or reviewing committees staffed by outside parties that are involved in the oversight of their CSR projects and by joining associations and other bodies that are engaged in the development and dissemination of best practices with respect to a CSR issue.[13]

When establishing plans for reporting and verification, it is useful to obtain and review copies of reports that have been done and published by comparable companies. Reports of larger companies are generally available on their corporate websites and extensive archives of past CSR-focused reports can be accessed through various online platforms such as CorporateRegister.com, a widely recognized global

---

[13] Id. at 79–80.

online directory of corporate responsibility reports. It is also important to have a good working understanding of well-known reporting and verification initiatives such as the GRI Standards; the AccountAbility AA1000 series; the United Nations Global Compact; and the International Auditing and Assurance Standards Board ISAE 3000 standard. Country-specific information is also available through professional organizations such as the Canadian Chartered Professional Accountants, which has published an extensive report on sustainability reporting in Canada.

The need to prepare reports relating to CSR activities creates another important process for companies: internal audits to ensure that the information included in the reports is accurate and complete. Auditing has long been a feature of financial reporting and companies reporting on CSR also need to engage in systematic, documented, periodic, and objective evaluation of how well the organization is doing with respect to implementing its CSR objectives and commitments and complying with relevant policies and procedures. Internal auditing for CSR requires a multidisciplinary team that includes engineers, scientists, auditors, and attorneys with the necessary experience in both the substantive issues and the art and science of the testing and sampling associated with audit practice. Auditing is not only data-driven but also includes insights from interviews, inspections, and simple observations of employees engaged in their day-to-day duties. Interactions with external stakeholders will be needed during the audit process to confirm their impressions of company activities. Some companies draw on outside audit specialists to serve as consultants to facilitate the audit process.

In addition to formal audits, directors and senior managers can and should regularly engage in other practices to ensure that the CSR program is being followed and make their own preliminary determination regarding the effectiveness of the program. For example, regular reports from middle managers that focus specifically on CSR initiatives should be solicited and reviewed and interviews with those managers should be conducted on a regular basis to elicit their opinions with respect to improvements in operational and reporting processes. Directors and senior managers should also increase their visibility by visiting and touring operating sites in order to observe how the CSR objectives are being pursued in practice. During those visits, time should be spent talking to employees to gauge their understanding of what is going on and how they feel about the initiatives and their particular roles. Directors and senior managers should also participate in other CSR-related events and activities such as meetings with employees, community groups, consumer advocates and key business partners.

Evaluating and Improving CSR Initiatives

Reporting and verification, both important in their own right, should also be seen as the catalyst for careful evaluation of the effectiveness and scope of the company's CSR initiatives and generation of ideas for modifying and improving those initiatives. Maon et al. recommended that in order to improve their CSR programs, companies should implement evaluation procedures based on measuring, verifying, and reporting in order to determine what is working well, why, and how to ensure that it will continue. In addition, companies need to investigate what is not working well and why this is the case, explore barriers to success and what can be changed to overcome these barriers and, if necessary, revisit original goals and make new ones.[14] Maon et al. explained that regular reviews and evaluations of the company's CSR activities are a means for keeping stakeholders informed of the progress and activities, thus providing visibility and transparency. The legitimacy of the review and evaluation process can be enhanced by involving external auditors and rigorous reporting that includes a comparison of the company's actual performance against previously established goals and targets. Maon et al. recommended that stakeholders be invited to verify the organization's CSR performance and report publicly on their findings.[15]

---

[14] F. Maon, V. Swaen and A. Lindgreen, *Mainstreaming the Corporate Responsibility Agenda: A Change Model Grounded in Theory and Practice* (IAG- Louvain School of Management Working Paper, 2008), 35–36 (citing P. Hohnen (Author) and J. Potts (Editor), *Corporate Social Responsibility: An Implementation Guide for Business* (Winnipeg, Canada: International Institute for Sustainable Development, 2007)).

[15] Id. at 36.

Hohnen and Potts admonished companies to use the results from the verification process, including information gathered from engaging stakeholders, to determine what is working well, why, and how to ensure that it continues to do so; investigate what is not working well and why not, to explore the barriers to success and what can be changed to overcome the barriers; assess what competitors and others in the sector are doing and have achieved; and revisit original goals and make new ones as necessary.[16] While some might ask why this is necessary when a detailed report has been prepared at great expense, it is important to distinguish the data and other information in the report from the process of thinking deeply about what the data and information really mean in practice. Questions that Hohnen and Potts suggested should be used in order to drive the evaluation process included the following:

- What worked well? In what areas did the company meet or exceed targets? Has the company celebrated its successes, an important way to continue motivating employees?
- Why did it work well? Were there factors within or outside the company that helped it meet its targets?
- What did not work well? In what areas did the company not meet its targets?
- Why were these areas problematic? Were there factors within or outside the company that made the process more difficult or created obstacles?
- What did the company learn from this experience? What should continue and what should be done differently?
- Is the company using the right reporting indicators? Are they aligned with the company's overall mission and CSR commitments?
- Is the company engaging with the right stakeholders?

---

[16] P. Hohnen (Author) and J. Potts (Editor), *Corporate Social Responsibility: An Implementation Guide for Business* (Winnipeg, Canada: International Institute for Sustainable Development, 2007), 73–74.

- Have the right persons for advancing CSR initiatives inside the company been identified and have they been given adequate support?
- Drawing on this knowledge, and information concerning new trends, what are the CSR priorities for the company in the coming year?
- Are there new CSR objectives?

Section 7.7 of ISO 26000 addresses the reasons and procedures for continuously reviewing and improving the organization's actions and practices related to CSR, noting that effective performance with respect to social responsibility depends in part on commitment, careful oversight, evaluation, and review of the activities undertaken, progress made, achievement of identified objectives, resources used, and other aspects of the organization's efforts. Regular monitoring and review of CSR performance ensure that an organization understands whether its strategies and programs are proceeding as intended and allows the organization to identify problems and issues and take remedial actions including changes in programs and shifts in the CSR issues that are given the greatest attention. While many of the monitoring and review activities are internal—tracking metrics on progress toward CSR-related goals tied to operational matters (e.g., reduction of CO_2 emissions)—consideration must also be given to the opinions and insights available from external stakeholders. ISO 26000 also points out that organizations must continuously review changing conditions or expectations, legal or regulatory developments affecting social responsibility, and new opportunities for enhancing its efforts on social responsibility.[17]

Evaluating the performance of CSR-related programs and activities begins with establishing and maintaining monitoring procedures. CSR is complex and the amount of data with respect to a particular issue or program can be overwhelming. As such, Section 7.7.2 of ISO 26000

---

[17] ISO 26000 Guidance on Social Responsibility (Geneva: International Organization for Standardization, 2010), 81.

counsels organizations to focus on those activities that are significant and seek to make the results of the monitoring easy to understand, reliable, timely, and responsive to stakeholders' concerns. Organizations can choose to conduct reviews at appropriate intervals, engage in benchmarking that includes comparing performance to comparable organizations, and obtain feedback from affected stakeholders. Performance evaluation can also be facilitated through the proper setting and use of targets and indicators, as afore-described in this chapter, in order to proper measure both qualitative and quantitative aspects of performance and progress and compare the current state of affairs to historical information.[18]

Section 7.7.4 of ISO 26000 addresses the important issue of verifying the reliability of the information collected during the review process and the manner in which such information is stored and managed. While standards and best practices regarding auditing qualitative and quantitative information relating to CSR, and the reports regarding such information that are distributed by organizations, are still evolving and have not yet reached the level of maturity associated with financial accounting and auditing, organizations should engage independent people or groups, either internal or external to the organization, to examine the ways in which data is collected, recorded, or stored, handled and used by the organization. ISO 26000 points out that reliability can be improved through good training of data collectors, clear accountability for data accuracy, direct feedback to individuals making errors, and data quality processes that compare reported data with past data and that from comparable situations.[19] While data reliability is obviously important for accurate internal reviews of performance, it is essential in those instances where organizations are required to provide performance data to governmental agencies and nongovernmental organizations.[20]

---

[18] Id. at 81–82.

[19] Id. at 82.

[20] Regulatory reporting may be required regarding emissions of CO_2 and other pollutants and as a condition for funding and participation in governmental programs and/or issuance and maintenance of environmental licenses and permits. Protection of personal information (i.e., financial and health information) is also both a legal issue and an important CSR concern. Id.

Section 7.7.3 of ISO 26000 calls on organizations to carry out reviews at appropriate intervals to determine how it is performing against its targets and objectives for social responsibility and to identify needed changes in the programs and procedures. Reviews not only look at progress against targets and indicators established at the beginning of a particular reporting period, but also involve comparisons against results from earlier reviews to assess overall progress. The review process is also a good way to focus attention on important intangibles relating to the CSR program—things that are admittedly difficult to measure—such as changes in attitudes relating to CSR throughout the organization and how well CSR is being implemented and integrated. Among the review questions suggested by ISO 26000 were the following[21]:

- Were objectives and targets achieved as envisioned?
- Did the strategies and processes suit the objectives?
- What worked and why? What did not work and why?
- Were the objectives appropriate?
- What could have been done better?
- Are all relevant persons involved?

An effort should be made to gather information from a variety of perspectives regarding these review questions including external stakeholders. The process should be documented and described in the organization's CSR reporting and communications and stakeholders should be informed about how the results of the review were used to make changes in CSR-related strategies and programs to improve performance.

There are several goals for the review process including collecting the information necessary for appropriate reporting and other communications regarding the organization's CSR activities. In addition, however, the results of the review should be used to identify and implement new ideas for improving the organization's performance on social responsibility and, as appropriate, making changes to the goals and targets of its CSR programs. An organization may decide that it is necessary to invest

---

[21] Id. at 82.

additional resources in a particular program and/or broaden the scope of a program to generate greater environmental or social impact. The review may also uncover new opportunities to deliver social value while expanding and improving the organization's line of products and services. The review process is a good way to ensure that there is regular dialogue with key stakeholders, since their views are essential to tracking CSR performance. Finally, measurement of CSR performance and progress toward CSR-related goals should be integrated with periodic assessments of the performance of senior executives, thus illustrating the seriousness of organizational commitment to CSR.[22]

Evaluations need to be done regularly, no less frequently than annually, and procedures should be established for tracking the results from evaluations year-on-year in order to gauge progress and identify any relevant patterns or trends. When conducting evaluations, input should be obtained from people throughout the organization as line-level employees may have very different impressions of CSR initiatives than managers higher up in the organizational structure. When small businesses conduct an evaluation, it need not be time-consuming. In fact, a good deal can be learned from having everyone in the company get together for a working meeting and planning session to go through and discuss each of the questions laid out earlier.

Certifications and Ratings Systems

Another way that organizations can measure and demonstrate their commitment to social and environmental responsibility is through participation in ratings agencies and ratings systems that have been created in order to give external stakeholders a means by which they can assess the social and environmental impact of the organization's activities. In order to participate in these systems, some of which actually offer opportunities for certification, organizations must be prepared to adjust their internal structures in order to comply with the requirements of the system and ensure that the information necessary for measurement can be collected, analyzed, and properly reported. While there are similarities among the

---

[22] Id. at 83.

most popular systems, there is still no universal standard and many of the systems operate without extensive efforts to verify or audit the information provided by organizations, although organizations should expect that they will be required to submit to site visits and renew their certifications on a regular basis.[23]

Perhaps the most well-known certification program is overseen by B Lab Company (B Lab), a Pennsylvania nonprofit corporation that administers certification as a Certified B Corp., which offers access to the Certified B Corporation logo often seen as being a "Good Housekeeping Seal of Approval" for sustainable businesses. In order to become "certified," a company must achieve a minimum verified score on a "B Impact Assessment" that assesses the overall impact of the company on its stakeholders taking into account various factors such as number of employees, sector, and location of the company's primary operations. The questions in the B Impact Assessment have by created and revised by the Standards Advisory Council, a group of independent experts in business and academia, and cover financial performance; suppliers; the impact of the business on all its stakeholders; best practices regarding mission, measurement and governance; and the company's "impact business model."

Companies that complete the B Impact Assessment will receive a B Impact Report that contains an overall score based on performance in three key impact areas (i.e., workers, community, and the environment) and will move on an assessment review and submission of supporting documentation. At this point, the focus will be on the operations of the company and demonstration of practice relating to the company's social and environmental impact. Additional steps in the assessment process include completion of a disclosure questionnaire, which allows companies to confidentially disclose to B Lab any sensitive practices, fines, and sanctions related to the company and its partners, and background checks by B Lab staff, which include a review of public records, news sources, and search engines for company names, brands, executives/founders, and other relevant topics.

---

[23] *Which Legal Structure is Right for My Social Enterprise?: A Guide to Establishing a Social Enterprise in the United States* (Thomson Reuters Foundation and Morrison & Foerster, September 2016), 111–112.

Around 10 percent of certified B corporations are randomly selected each year for an in-depth site review, which takes place either in person or virtually and typically takes 6 to 10 hours depending on the size and scope of the business. Site reviews are considered to be a crucial step for verifying the requirements of the Certified B Corp. certification and confirming the accuracy of the responses of the specific company. Companies wishing to maintain their Certified B Corp. certification are required to update their assessment every two years by providing additional documentation and achieving a minimum score on the impact assessment. Recertification requirements provide assurances that companies are continuing to engage in a high level of impact with their stakeholders even as their businesses grow or change. The recertification process also provides companies with opportunities to set their own internal improvement goals against B Lab standards and benchmark their performance over time.[24]

Various product, safety, and environmental certifications are available depending on the industry and activities of the organization. For example, UL (www.ul.com) helps companies demonstrate safety, confirm compliance, enhance sustainability, manage transparency, deliver quality and performance, strengthen security, protect brand reputation, build workplace excellence, and advance societal well-being through a range of services including inspection, advisory services, education and training, testing, auditing and analytics, certification software solutions, and marketing claim verification. UL's Sustainability Quotient (SQ®) Program provides organizations with the opportunity to achieve third party sustainability certification for their whole enterprise, demonstrating clear market leadership, and a commitment to environmental stewardship at every level of business operations. The SQ® Program is a comprehensive system of assessing, rating, and certifying the sustainability initiatives of corporations. With a focus on the environment, governance, workforce, customers/suppliers, and community engagement/human rights, the SQ® Program promotes the adoption of a standardized language and

---

[24] For complete information about becoming a Certified B Corp., see the B Lab website at http://www.bcorporation.net/ (which is the primary source of the summary description in this section) and R. Honeyman, *The B Corp Handbook: How to Use Business as a Force for Good* (Oakland, CA: Berrett-Koehler Publishers, 2014).

rating platform for corporate sustainability. UL also tests and certifies products, processes, and materials against current environmental standards and maintains a database of validated and certified products that can be accessed by industry professional and consumers.

Costs to organizations for attempting to comply with certification programs and standards will vary and consideration should be given to fees that must be paid to the agency and the investments that must be made in order to fulfill the agency's requirements. Organizations must also consider the potential impact of participating in a particular rating or certification program, or complying with a formal reporting regime, on the organization's governance or regulatory obligations depends on the program. However, the costs and disruptions to traditional operating procedures must be balanced against the benefits of being able to provide potential investors and stakeholders with reliable information to accurately assess the social impact such companies make, thus making it easier for organizations to raise capital from investors seeking to support socially responsible ventures and attract employees and customers want to do business with companies that are having a positive social and environmental impact.[25]

In addition to formal assessment, feedback on sustainability initiatives comes from other groups who watch and monitor industry activities and the behaviors of individual companies. Shareholders have become much more aggressive in questioning the activities of management and companies can also expect to be scrutinized by labor unions, consumer activists, environmentalists. and other community groups. The possibility of government regulation has often motivated industries to "self-regulate" by adopting standards and codes of conduct to be followed by industry members. One place to look for ideas about measuring sustainability is in the financial community where various indexes and other measures of corporate performance on various sustainability-related criteria (e.g., governance, human resource management, health and safety, environmental protection, and community development) have been developed to assist

---

[25] *Which Legal Structure is Right for My Social Enterprise?: A Guide to Establishing a Social Enterprise in the United States* (Thomson Reuters Foundation and Morrison & Foerster, September 2016), 114–115.

public and private investors, including mutual fund managers and venture capitalists, in making investment decisions. Interest in measurement has exploded as more investment capital is being set aside for "socially responsible investment."

It is important to understand how a particular index defines sustainability and CSR. Many earlier indexes focused on screening out companies that operated in undesirable or risky industries; however, as time went by the metrics became broader and more sophisticated and included positive factors such as leadership approaches, planning processes, and management practices in areas such as governance, social impact, and the environment. Notable examples of sustainability indexes include the Dow Jones Sustainability indices and the MSCI ESG indexes. An extensive library of reports and self-reported climate change, water, and forest-risk data is available through the CDP (www.cdp.net), which works with companies, investors, and governments on issues and projects relating to environmental risks.[26] Indices of sustainability and CSR have been supplemented by efforts to list and rank the most socially responsible companies. For example, Corporate Knights releases an annual list of the "Top 100 Most Sustainable Corporations in the World."

---

[26] P. Hohnen (Author) and J. Potts (Editor), *Corporate Social Responsibility: An Implementation Guide for Business* (Winnipeg, Canada: International Institute for Sustainable Development, 2007), 10.

About the Author

The author of this book is **Alan S. Gutterman**, whose prolific output of practical guidance and tools for legal and financial professionals, managers, entrepreneurs, and investors has made him one of the best-selling individual authors in the global legal publishing marketplace. His cornerstone work, *Business Transactions Solution*, is an online-only product available and featured on Thomson Reuters' Westlaw, the world's largest legal content platform, which includes almost 200 book-length modules covering the entire lifecycle of a business. Alan has also authored or edited over 90 books on sustainable entrepreneurship, leadership and management, business law and transactions, international law and business, and technology management for a number of publishers including Thomson Reuters, Practical Law, Kluwer, Routledge, Aspatore, Oxford, Quorum, ABA Press, Aspen, Sweet & Maxwell, Euromoney, Harvard Business Publishing, CCH, and BNA. Alan is currently a partner of GCA Law Partners LLP in Mountain View, CA (www.gcalaw.com) and has extensive experience as a partner and senior counsel with internationally recognized law firms counseling small and large business enterprises in the areas of general corporate and securities matters, venture capital, mergers and acquisitions, international law and transactions, strategic business alliances, technology transfers, and intellectual property, and has also held senior management positions with several technology-based businesses including service as the chief legal officer of a leading international distributor of IT products headquartered in Silicon Valley and as the chief operating officer of an emerging broadband media company. He has been an adjunct faculty member at several colleges and universities and has also launched the Sustainable Entrepreneurship Project (www.seproject.org) to teach and support individuals and companies, both startups and mature firms, seeking to create and build sustainable businesses based on purpose, innovation, shared value, and respect for people and planet. He has also launched a projects relating to ageism.

Index

Aspirational commitments, 90, 91
Assessment process, 5, 12, 13, 34, 35,
    42, 49–50, 67–69, 78, 89,
    113, 158–160
  economic, social, and
    environmental impacts,
    59–61
  leadership team, 50–52, 55
  legal and regulatory standards,
    53–55
  organization's size and
    circumstances, 62
  prioritization, 64–65
  review process, 55–57
  stakeholder analysis, 57–59
  subjects and issues, 62–65

Balanced scorecard (BSC) approach,
    86–87
Barney, J., 21
BASF SE, 119, 120
Being heard, 32
Being informed, 32
Bertels, S., 121, 122
B Impact Assessment, 158
B Lab Company (B Lab), 158
Boston Consulting Group (BCG),
    119
Bristol-Myers Squibb, 99, 100
Business plan, 128–130

Canadian Business for Social
    Responsibility (CBSR), 122
Canadian Chartered Professional
    Accountants, 151
CDP (www.cdp.net), 161
Ceres Roadmap, 94–96, 147
Certifications, 157–161
Certified B Corp, 158, 159
Chief sustainability officers (CSOs),
    117–118
Choice making, 32

Commitments, 89–93
  communication, 108–109
  consultation, revision, and
    publication, 107–108
  guidelines to employees, 95–96
  and instruments, 94
  monitoring process, 109–110
  organizational, 97–98, 100–102
  performance, 105–107
  preliminary draft, 103–105
  roadmap, 94–96
  scanning process, 93–96
  stakeholders, 98–100
  working group, 102–103
Commitment statement, 91
Communications, 13
Community, 39–40, 85
Community engagement, 42–43,
    133, 135, 159
Competitors, 41
Compliance, 101
Corporate culture, 15
CorporateRegister.com, 150–151
Corporate social responsibility (CSR),
    7–9, 34, 49–50, 67–69
  actions and activities, 78–82
  assessment (See Assessment process)
  balanced scorecard, 86–87
  business case, 82
  commitments (See Commitments)
  definition of, 52–53
  direction, approach, and focus
    areas, 83–86
  implementation plan (See
    Implementation plan)
  initiative (See Initiative)
  ISO 26000, 75–78
  leadership team, 50–52, 55, 68, 74,
    79–81
  research on, 74–75
  senior management and employees,
    69–70

and sustainability strategy, 10–16, 161
SWOT analysis, 70–73
Corruption and bribery, 101
Credibility, 150
Cultural forces, 45–48

Data reliability, 155
Debarliev, S., 18, 21
Decision making, 4, 10, 17, 19, 32, 52, 55, 67–69, 97, 111, 125–128, 135
Demographic forces, 45–48
Disclosure in Financial Filings, 148
Distributors, 33–35
Diversity, 96
Dow Jones Sustainability indices, 161
Drucker, P., 22
Due diligence process, 61–62

Eccles, R., 123, 124
Economic forces, 43–44
Education, 32
Employee development, 101
Employee health and safety, 101
Employees, 95, 100
Employee support, 135–137
Environment, 25–28, 85, 100
    forces (See General environmental forces)
    specific (See Specific environment)
    and strategic business, 27–28
Environmental forces, 44–45
Ethical purchasing and human rights, 101
Evaluation, 152–157
External communications, 141

Flexibility, 72

Galbraith, J., 122
General Electric (GE), 84
General environmental forces, 43
    demographic, cultural, and social forces, 45–48
    economic forces, 43–44

political and environmental forces, 44–45
    technological forces, 44
Global communities, 100
Global Reporting Initiative (GRI), 92, 132–134
Goals and objectives, 5–6

Healthy environment, 32
Heidrick and Struggles, 117
Hohmann, P., 9, 12, 52, 57, 68, 69, 80, 83, 89, 90, 93, 99, 125, 127, 128, 132, 134–136, 153

Implementation plan, 13, 15, 111–112, 131
    business plan, 128–130
    decision-making structure, 125–128
    development, 112–116
    and employees, 135–137
    external communications, 141
    Global Reporting Initiative, 132–134
    internal communications, 138–141
    internal organizational structure, 116–118
    management system, 118–120
    qualitative and quantitative performance, 132
    strategy and, 114–116
    sustainability-oriented organizational culture, 120–124
Improvement, 145, 152–157
Initiative, 143–146
    certifications and ratings systems, 157–161
    evaluating and improving, 152–157
    reporting and verification, 146–152
Input environment, 29
Internal communications, 138–141
Internal environment, 26, 27, 29
Internal management control, 130–131
Internal organizational structure, 116–118
Internationalization, 47–48

International multistakeholder
    processes (IMPs), 93
ISO 26000, 37, 39, 61–64, 75–78,
    148–150, 154–155

Kellogg Company, 84–86
Key performance indicators (KPIs),
    107

Labor practices, 35–38
Labor unions, 36, 45
Learn, 145

Macro-environment, 26, 27
Maignan, I., 97
Management participation, 3–5
Maon, F., 10, 97, 152
Marketplace, 85
Measure, 145
Mission statement, 5
MIT Sloan Management Review, 119
Monitoring, 6, 15–16, 109–110
    and evaluation, 20–21
MSCI ESG indexes, 161

Neilson, G., 22, 23
Network for Business Sustainability
    (NBS), 121–122

Operations, 95
Organization
    costs to, 160
    CSR commitments, 97–98,
        100–102
    domain, 26, 29, 30, 33, 35, 41,
        43, 44
    environment, 25–26
    size and circumstances, 62
    social responsibilities, 61–62
    sustainability-oriented, 120–124
Output environment, 29

Patients and customers, 100
PepsiCo, 51
Performance, 14
Performance measurement system,
    144–145
Plan–Do–Check–Improve, 12–13

Policies and objectives, 14
Policy statement, 91
Political forces, 44–45
Political stability, 46
Potts, J., 9, 12, 52, 57, 68, 69, 80, 83,
    89, 90, 93, 99, 125, 127, 128,
    132, 134–136, 153
Preliminary draft, 103–105
Prescriptive commitments, 90
Privatization, 47, 64–65
Product quality and safety to
    customers, 101
Products and services, 95

Qualitative performance, 132
Quantitative performance, 132

Rangan, K., 8, 9
Ratings systems, 157–161
Recertification process, 159
Recruitment, 95
Redress, 32
Regulators, 38
Report, 145
Reporting, 146–152
Resource use and waste management,
    101
Review process, 55–57, 156

Safety, 32
Scope and Content, 148
Shareholders, 100
Social forces, 45–48
Social responsibility, 39, 125
Special interest groups, 40–41
Specific environment, 29–30
    communities, 39–40
    competitors, 41
    labor practices, 35–38
    products, services, and customers,
        30–32
    regulators, 38
    special interest groups, 40–41
    stakeholder engagement, 41–43
    suppliers and distributors, 33–35
Stakeholder
    analysis, 14, 57–59
    CSR commitments, 98–100

engagement, 12, 41–43, 57–58, 69, 79, 91, 99, 115, 133, 134, 150
Standards Advisory Council, 158
Standards for Disclosure, 148
Star Model, 122
Strategic planning, 7–10, 18–19
    CSR and sustainability strategy, 10–16
    definitions and objectives, 2–3
    effectiveness, 21–22
    efforts, 18–19
    elements of, 5–7
    management participation, 3–5
    monitoring and evaluation, 20–21
    products and services, 30–31
    skills, 19–20
    socially responsible companies, 31–32
    strategy execution, 22–24
    sustainable business practices, 16–18
Strategy, 13–15, 68
    execution, 22–24
    and implementation plan, 114–116
Strengths, Weaknesses, Opportunities, and Threats (SWOT) analysis, 5, 70–73
Sukle, B., 18, 21
Suppliers, 33–35, 115–116
Supply chain, 95
    ethical purchasing and human rights, 101
    management, 33–35, 116, 135
Sustainability, 7–17, 51, 58, 82, 84, 94–100, 104–106, 117, 119, 120, 150, 159–161

business practices, 16–18
development principles, 13–16
leadership, 94, 147
lifestyles, 96
organizational culture, 120–124
strategy, 10–16
Sustainability Quotient (SQ®) Program, 159–160
Sustainable Development Goals (SDGs), 96

Tactical plan, 6
Task environment, 26, 27, 29
Technological forces, 44
Technology, 102
Time period, 6–7
Training and development, 95–96
Transportation and logistics, 95
Triple bottom line, 10

UL (www.ul.com), 159, 160
UN Global Compact, 11–13, 53, 76
UN Guidelines for Consumer Protection, 31–32
Universal design, promotion of, 32

Vehicles for Disclosure, 148
Verification, 146–152
Verification and Assurance, 148
Visions, 94–95

Whistleblower protection, 129
Wolk, A., 144–145
Working group, 102–103
Workplace, 85
World Trade Organization, 47

OTHER TITLES IN THE ENVIRONMENTAL AND SOCIAL SUSTAINABILITY FOR BUSINESS ADVANTAGE COLLECTION

Robert Sroufe, Duquesne University, Editor

- *Sustainability Leader in a Green Business Era* by Amr E. Sukkar
- *Managing Sustainability* by John Friedman
- *Human Resource Management for Organizational Sustainability* by Radha R. Sharma
- *Climate Change Management* by Huong Ha
- *Social Development Through Benevolent Business* by Kalyan Sankar Mandal
- *Developing Sustainable Supply Chains to Drive Value, Volume I* by Robert P. Sroufe and Steven A. Melnyk
- *Developing Sustainable Supply Chains to Drive Value, Volume II* by Robert P. Sroufe and Steven A. Melnyk
- *ISO 50001 Energy Management Systems* by Johannes Kals
- *Feasibility Analysis for Sustainable Technologies* by Scott R. Herriott
- *The Role of Legal Compliance in Sustainable Supply Chains, Operations, and Marketing* by John Wood
- *Change Management for Sustainability* by Huong Ha
- *The Thinking Executive's Guide to Sustainability* by Kerul Kassel
- *A Primer on Sustainability* by Ronald Whitfield and Jeanne McNett
- *IT Sustainability for Business Advantage* by Brian Moore
- *Developing Sustainable Supply Chains to Drive Value* by Robert Sroufe and Steven Melnyk

Concise and Applied Business Books

The Collection listed above is one of 30 business subject collections that Business Expert Press has grown to make BEP a premiere publisher of print and digital books. Our concise and applied books are for...

- Professionals and Practitioners
- Faculty who adopt our books for courses
- Librarians who know that BEP's Digital Libraries are a unique way to offer students ebooks to download, not restricted with any digital rights management
- Executive Training Course Leaders
- Business Seminar Organizers

Business Expert Press books are for anyone who needs to dig deeper on business ideas, goals, and solutions to everyday problems. Whether one print book, one ebook, or buying a digital library of 110 ebooks, we remain the affordable and smart way to be business smart. For more information, please visit www.businessexpertpress.com, or contact sales@businessexpertpress.com.

www.ingramcontent.com/pod-product-compliance
Lightning Source LLC
Chambersburg PA
CBHW061314220326
41599CB00026B/4868

* 9 7 8 1 9 5 2 5 3 8 9 4 0 *